ENCOUNTERING MYSTERY
IN THE WILDERNESS:
ONE WOMAN'S VISION QUEST

SOR JUANA PRESS

Sor Juana Press is a project of Santuario Sisterfarm, a nonprofit organization rooted in the Texas Hill Country and grounded in the rich multi-cultural legacy of the Borderlands. Founded in 2002, Santuario Sisterfarm inspirits the work of transforming human relationships with Earth and other humans by moving from dominance to co-creative partnerships, drawing on insights from wisdom traditions, nature, the new science, and women's ways. Santuario Sisterfarm advances its mission by cultivating diversity—biodiversity and cultural diversity.

Sor Juana Press is dedicated to publishing the works of women—particularly women of color and women religious—on topics rooted in women's

spirituality and relation-ship with Earth, *la Tierra, nuestra madre.*

The Press invokes the name and honors the memory of Sor Juana Inés de la Cruz (1648-1695), a Mexican nun, scholar, poet, playwright, musician, and scientist—a woman with a *sed de conocer* (thirst for knowing)—who was silenced for advocating women's education. She is the first writer in the Americas to speak out in favor of a woman's right to learn and express concern about human depredation of the environment.

Other Books in the "Dominican Women on Earth" Series

EARTH SPIRITUALITY: IN THE CATHOLIC AND DOMINICAN TRADITIONS by Sharon Therese Zayac, O.P. (Issue No. 1, June 2003).

PERMACULTURE: FINDING OUR OWN VINES AND FIG TREES by Carol Coston, O.P. (Issue No. 2, August 2003).

EARTH, OUR HOME: BIBLICAL WITNESS IN THE HEBREW SCRIPTURES by Sarah Ann Sharkey, O.P. (Issue No. 3, February 2004).

ENCOUNTERING MYSTERY IN THE WILDERNESS:
ONE WOMAN'S VISION QUEST

Margaret Galiardi, O.P.

CONVERSATIO

Dominican Women on Earth

Issue No.4   April 2004

SOR JUANA PRESS

San Antonio, Texas

Edited by Elise D. García and Carol Coston, O.P.

Photograph on cover and p. 56 by Dr. Lloyd Glenn Ingles. Copyright © 1999 California Academy of Sciences.

Photographs on pp. 22 and 35 by Anne Stine; on p. 47 by Joe Bostic

Cover and book design by Susan E. Klein of Sister Creek Studios, San Antonio, Texas. (www.sistercreekstudios.com)

Printed by Crumrine Printers, Inc., San Antonio, Texas

This book is printed with soy inks on 100% post-consumer recycled paper, processed chorine-free, supplied by Dolphin Blue, a Dallas, Texas-based company specializing in environmentally responsible office products. (www.dolphinblue.com)

ISBN 0-9740243-3-3
ISSN 1543-978X

www.santuariosisterfarm.org

TABLE OF CONTENTS

ABOUT THE AUTHOR

Margaret Galiardi, O.P. has been a member of the Dominican Sisters of Amityville (New York) since 1964. Her ministries through the years have included teaching grade school, working in parishes, and coordinating programs for homeless persons. Margaret spent almost a decade working at the Intercommunity Center for Justice and Peace in Manhattan, while in the evenings residing in a convent that was also a shelter for women who were homeless, battered, or released from prison and their children. Margaret served as Theological Curriculum Coordinator for the lay leadership training program of the Diocese of Rockville Center, and lived in community with undocumented persons at the Oscar Romero Inn.

In June 1995, Margaret was elected to the governing team of her Congregation as Director of Ministry. At the same time, in addition to holding the responsibilities of this position, Margaret responded to an invitation to serve as the Co-Promoter of Justice for North America for the worldwide Dominican Order. This entailed membership on the Dominican International Commission for Justice, Peace, and the Integrity of Creation, as well as travel to Bolivia, El Salvador, Guatemala, Nicaragua, Cuba, Dominican Republic, Italy, France, Spain, Belgium, Israel, Iraq, Hong Kong, and the Philippines.

Most recently, Margaret has become engaged in focusing on the inner consciousness of humans and the role it plays in generating global imbalance. This focus centers her work on an Earth-based eco-spirituality that finds expression in her present position at Siena Spirituality Center in Water Mill, New York, where Margaret serves as Director of a sabbatical program premised on insights from the New Cosmology and as staff person for ecological concerns.

SHARING THE JOURNEY

My mother often told me, "Every day—even when it was cold—I would take you and your sister out for a walk along the water."

"The water" was the Brooklyn side of the Verrazano Bay which leads, alternately, into the New York harbor and out into the Atlantic Ocean. It was not far from here that was I born in December of 1946. It was, I am sure, those daily excursions along the shore that are responsible for my love of the water and all things expansive.

A family move to Queens when I was about six years old brought us to this teeming borough. Now home to millions of people, Queens was then an expanse of open fields (we called them lots) and a paradise for me. I was constantly outside, chasing rabbits and catching polliwogs in ponds. I even carried a full-grown rooster in my arms for several blocks when a friend's dad said I could have it if my parents agreed. (Of course, they didn't!)

Almost every evening, we as a family sat on the front stoop of our home. The site of the Empire State building and the New York City skyline, soon to be obscured by buildings, thrilled my mother. My dad, sister Joan (my senior by three years), and I always played the game of watching for the first star to appear. Whoever spotted it quickly recited the verse,

"I see the first star, the first star sees me. God bless the first star, God bless me."

These early experiences soon faded into the background of my life as the streets were paved and homes were built on every available parcel of land. My paradise in the nat-ural world had disappeared. My friends and I trans-ferred our allegiance to school with all the projects and extracurricular activities that were typical of Catholic parish life in late 1950s and early '60s. I loved sports and participated in the few activities that were open to girls—track and basketball. My good friend Pat's dad coached the boys' baseball team, so every Saturday morning we were off to the games. She and I both learned how to do official baseball league scoring and would take turns performing this important task. Although I participated in the "Girls Club," sewing and the like just didn't have the same appeal for me.

I enjoyed school and, from as early as I can remember, read everything I could. My elementary education passed quickly, and before I knew it I was attending All Saints, an all-girls Catholic high school in Brooklyn. I simply loved every minute of it, no doubt because there was a true family spirit between the faculty and the students. I spent hours after school working on the school paper and preparing for my role in the annual play. It was, I believe, the sisters' sheer joy and love of life that got me thinking about entering the convent. Of course, I was dating at the time and wasn't happy about the fact that the two choices weren't compatible. There were no athletic offerings at my high school so I continued playing basketball for my parish until late in my junior year. I switched to cheerleading then because I thought it would be more beneficial to my social life.

It was at Christmas Eve Mass in 1963 (which I attended with my boyfriend) when I secretly decided I would give convent life a try. Much to the chagrin of my parents (my mother, in particular), on the twelfth day of September in 1964, I became a "candidate," as it is now called, in the congregation of the Dominican Sisters of Amityville, New York. The Second Vatican Council was drawing to a close but its challenges to women's religious communities were yet to be embraced. Consequently, the "religious life" I entered still retained all of the hallmarks of the tradition. At the heart of it all, clear to me from the beginning, was a sense of relatedness with Holy Mystery—*a sense that life was going somewhere*. If you had told me then that some thirty-five years later it would be the Kit Fox (also called the Desert Fox) that would usher me into a deeper realization of this conviction, I would never have believed you! But now I am getting ahead of myself.

Like many young women who entered religious life in their late teenage years, I had some growing to do in order to embrace full womanhood. Religious life proved to be a place where I could do just that. There was time for reading and reflecting and wise women (and some men, too!) who taught me how to pray, acted as mentors, and helped me negotiate the passages involved in coming into my own.

As was the norm at that time, upon completion of my formation, I was sent out to teach school. I loved the years I taught intermediate and junior high school. The vibrancy of youth met my own passion for life. I was industrious in my preparations and teaching, but most of all I had fun with the students and felt a genuine affection for them.

I will never forget the morning a fierce snow storm hit the Huntington, Long Island area where I was teaching. One wall of the classroom was framed by a huge glass window looking out at the street. The eighth-grade students, mesmerized by the falling snow and its steady accumulation, were not paying a bit of attention to the day's lesson. I, too, kept trying to grab a peek as I went on and on about something. Finally, I realized it was a losing battle. All of us wanted to watch the pine trees gently bow as they accepted the coat of white offered by Mother Nature. So I directed the students to clear their desks, turn toward the window, and gleefully announced that we would all look at the snow for the next ten minutes and then return to the tasks at hand. It backfired! The students thought I was disap-pointed by their lack of attention and wouldn't take their eyes away from me. I never did get to watch the snow!

JOURNEYING TO THE HEART OF THE MATTER

My years in the classroom were short, though not due to any unhappiness on my part. Rather, I began to see that the education of the young, critical as it is, seemed so often to get side-tracked by the adults who conveyed to the young the very attitudes and values that needed to be challenged. What surfaced in me was a desire to devote my energy to what seemed to me to be the heart of the matter. This instinct, although I could not know it at the time, was to follow me throughout my life and lead to many a transition and challenge.

Initially, it took me to involvement with adults, first in the area of parent and teacher education and then as pastoral associate at Our Lady Queen of Martyrs parish on the north fork of Suffolk County, Long Island. Parish work fit me like a glove! Most of all, I loved the variety of it. One part of the day found me exploring the meaning of faith with adults; another, preparing teachers to instruct children. Then it was on to visit people in their homes, and sometimes hospitals and nursing homes as well. The people of this parish, in their generosity and hunger for a vibrant relationship with God, taught me what the second Vatican Council meant when it proclaimed that Church is the "People of God." I felt humbled and enriched by sharing their personal joys and struggles; I was deeply moved by their courage in the face of life's tragedies.

A second engagement in pastoral ministry in the Diocese of Richmond, Virginia followed. This was a great big stretch for me: For the first time in my adult life, I was leaving, with some sense of permanency, my 120-mile Long Island home; I found myself in an area of the country where Catholics, a minority, were greeted with fear and suspicion, if not outright hostility. While I honestly wanted to embrace the challenge, I found that I was fearful. I can still remember my feelings as I stepped onto the plane that was to carry me and a dear friend and sister in community, Jeanne Clark, to our new home. Again, although I could not know it at the time, fear in the face of challenge was another instinctual reaction of mine that was to follow me throughout my life journey.

Most memorable from these years in the South was my involvement with a young couple who, some years before my arrival, tragically lost a child in a drowning accident at the parish picnic. Told of this tragedy, I was delighted to learn that the couple had decided to have another child. From the looks of the mom, the baby's arrival was imminent.

One morning I received a frantic call from our parish secretary. The hospital had called. The couple's child had been born, a girl, and a priest was needed quickly. But all of the priests in the area were four hours away at a diocesan gathering of clergy.

Instinctively, I got in my car and was on the way to the hospital. During the fifteen-minute drive to the hospital I imagined every possible reason for the request, and hoped and prayed that I could at least be a healing presence. I arrived at the hospital to learn that the baby had been born with a fatal blood disorder that prevented oxygen from being carried throughout her body. She was on a respirator. They were waiting for someone to baptize her. Upon removal from the machine, she would certainly die.

I can still hear the words that Harold, the father, uttered on greeting me. "Not once, but twice, I must lose a child." Together, we baptized a beautiful little girl. My hands shook and tears ran down my face as I poured water over the head of this infant. Afterwards, we went together to tell Bea, his wife, that their child had passed away.

ENGAGING IN SYSTEMIC CHANGE

I really loved parish ministry. As I embraced it more fully, though, the clerical system rose up to greet me. I have no wish to go into the gory details—but believe me they were that. Suffice it to say that the hierarchical, male-dominated clerical system and I did not make good companions, and so I moved on. But I managed to process this experience in a way that led me outward: I made the connections between my own experiences as a woman in the Church and the world-wide oppression of women, people of color, low-income persons, and the peoples and nations of the South. I count this as one of the greatest blessings of my life as I know women, better than myself, who were overwhelmed by the experience of clericalism and subsequently withdrew from involvement with public issues of any sort for their own physical and mental health.

It was precisely the gift of my processing this experience in the way I did that opened up my next ministerial experience. In 1979, I happily learned of the Intercommunity Center for Justice and Peace in New York City, a coalition of religious congregations, committed to implementing Catholic social teaching on the systemic level. I began an internship with the organization and on its completion, took their only available position—in fundraising and development. The thought of raising funds seemed daunting at first, but my desire to do the work of justice was stronger than my fear of raising money.

I soon learned that in order to do the job successfully I had to develop an in-depth understanding of the issues around the nuclear arms race, the wars in Central America, and justice education to name a few. These were exciting years, as the fruits of Latin American liberation theology and feminist studies were becoming available. Having always been an avid reader, I gobbled up everything I could get my hands on. A staff of extremely capable women at the Center and wonderful opportunities for on-the-job-training had the effect of enhancing my analytical skills. Together with Rosalie Carvin, C.S.J., Darlene Cuccinello, Margaret Dowling, S.C., Barbara Glendon, O.S.U., Kathleen Kanet, R.S.H.M., Regina Murphy, S.C., Eleanor O'Doherty, S.C., and Pat Wolf,

R.S.M., I was exposed to a framework and method-ology for uncovering the systemic causes of the ills that plague our world. Fond memories of Jesuit Tom Clarke instructing us in how to move through the Faith Praxis Cycle (or the Theological Reflection Circle) remain vivid in my memory. International travel, a unique learning experience, also came into my life at this point. I visited war-torn Central America: Nicaragua, Guatemala, and El Salvador, and began learning that the "Third" world is really the "Two-Thirds" world.

Yet another opportunity presented itself at this time that was to change my life. A friend and sister in community, Barbara Wetenko, invited several of us to her convent home in East Flatbush in Brooklyn, New York. It was a new model of religious commu-nity founded by Brentwood Josephite Sister Elaine Roulet. Called Providence House, the big old con-vent in which the sisters lived also served as a shel-ter for homeless women, battered women and their children, as well as women recently released from prison. I can recall being very quiet that evening dur-ing dinner as the realization broke through to me that I wanted to share in this style of life.

With little difficulty, things fell into place and I moved in. This meant that during the day I was working to change the systems that were (and still are) the cause of poverty and oppression in our world, and in the evening I was living with women and children who were its victims. Although some friends warned against burnout, I found the combination enormously energizing and life-giving. These were the Reagan years. When I was ready to give up on systems change, I returned home in the evening to have dinner with those who suffered the most from the system's malfunctioning, and my determination to keep going was renewed. When I became exasperated with the behaviors of society's poorest, I gained new understanding of the depths to which systems wound people, and deeper levels of compassion were born in me.

The thread I would not let go of throughout all of these experiences, was my search for the deepest level at which to work—the cause/s which, if addressed, would move things in different direction.

Perhaps, I thought, if I were to spend time in the "developing world," I would internalize a different kind of consciousness. Perhaps I would learn from the people what it meant to have hope in what appeared to be hopeless situations. Perhaps I would learn why and how those with so little live out of a sense of abundance, while we in the "first world," who have so much, live out of a sense of scarcity.

I decided I would celebrate my twenty-fifth year in the community by living and working among the people of Guatemala. I was very excited and minimally fearful, despite the fact that the country was in the midst of a civil war. I had made careful plans, arranging to engage in a ministry that involved working in a new parish with a sister who had lived in the country for years. I would begin with language study and on the weekends connect with some of the sisters who live in the region, all to help me prepare for my new ministry. There was nothing to be concerned about, I assured the congregation and my friends and family.

Little did I know what would await me a few hours later when I boarded the plane to Guatemala that morning in July 1989. On arrival, I learned that due to a series of unforeseen events, all of my plans for ministry had fallen through! It evidently never dawned on the person who was my primary contact that it might have been good to alert me to this fact *before* I left the United States. So, there I was in the middle of a country in the midst of civil war, with halting Spanish and no clear plan of what to do after I completed language school.

People were very kind and two local communities of women religious—Rachael Sena and Evette Gioannetti from the Eucharistic Missionaries of St. Dominic, and Miriam Oliveros and Antonette (now, Theresa) Macey from the Houston Dominicans—opened their doors to me and warmly welcomed me into their midst. But no matter how much I wanted to stay on, even trying to explore other ministerial options, it became increasingly obvious that things were not working out. After four tortuous months, I made peace with the fact that I needed to return to the States. In the midst of great sadness and disappointment, I understood that working at the level of root causes of what most deeply afflicts our society often entails a powerlessness not of our own choosing.

Processing this experience was a challenge. My years of work at the Intercommunity Center had convinced me that if change on behalf of a more just society did not happen at the level of societal systems, we would simply be "rearranging the deck chairs on the Titanic." On the other hand, my years at Providence House and the brief but powerful experience in Guatemala, showed me that it was critical that low-income and other marginalized persons be involved in making societal change happen.

I decided to focus my energies on ministries where I could "braid" these insights together and accepted a position as Homelessness Prevention Coordinator with the Inter-faith Nutrition Network, an organization of soup kitchens and shelters on Long Island. Following this, I returned to Providence House, this time working out of its central office as a staff member facilitating an "After-Care" program. I hated the name of the program yet loved its central focus. In a team with two formerly homeless and dually addicted women, Robin and Max, we set about creating supportive networks for women, who after being in the "homeless system" had finally found places to live.

This was rich and rewarding work in which I received far more than I gave. In particular, I remember the long hours of mutual learning with Robin and Max, as together we sought to find ways for women to discover their own inner strength and live independently of "the system." Underneath it all, though, a couple of questions persisted: Where will our culture find the impetus for the deep transformation that is needed? What involvements will foster the radical change of values that will jump-start the re-shaping of society? No doubt much evil had been prevented by all the good work done on behalf of social justice. In my heart of hearts, though, it was becoming increasingly clear that, for me, something was still missing.

While moving forward with my involvements, I pursued these questions. I continued reading the liberation theologies: Latin American, Mujerista, American Black, Womanist, and Feminist from different continents. Next, I found myself drawn into Ecological and Eco-feminist theology. The work of Passionist "geologian" Thomas Berry fell into my hands. That led me to physicist Brian Swimme's writing and on to the lectures of Caldwell Dominican Sister Miriam Therese MacGillis.

As I turned all of this over in my heart, my sisters in community called me to serve on the governing board (then called the "Leadership Team") of my congregation, as Director of Ministry. It was June of 1995. Once again, I was to work with a group of extraordinarily talented women: Amityville Dominicans Mary Butler, Joan Cahill, Fran Gorman, Mary Hughes, Marge McGregor, Chris Sammons, Cathy Smith, and Barbara Suessmann.

As I was settling into the position, my secretary informed me one morning that I had a fax from Rome. I laughed, thinking it was a joke. She persisted. In her hand was a fax from Timothy Radcliff, then Master of the Dominican Order. I was being asked to accept the position of North American Co-Promoter of Justice for the Dominican Order. It was, of course, a position that would be added to my already more-than-fulltime job.

The fax sat on my desk for several days. It was a decision that I felt I needed to make carefully, as I had significant congregational obligations. In the end, I realized that accepting the position would serve not only the Order but also my own congregation, as it would enhance the sisters' identity as members of the worldwide Dominican Order.

The combined responsibilities of the two positions gave me much to ponder—most of which I was not free to share with anyone. I began taking very long walks, oftentimes in the pre-dawn light. I couldn't have put words on it then, but now I know that Earth, in all her numinosity, was becoming a living companion.

The Promoter's job entailed periodic trips to Rome for meetings of the International Commission for Justice, Peace, and (what was latter added) the Care of Creation. Amidst a plethora of very serious issues that found their way onto the agenda of the Commission, the suffering of the people of Iraq rose to the surface for me.

"I Have Family in Iraq"

Two things came together in a very powerful way. On the one hand, I was a citizen of the country whose government was enforcing, under United Nations auspices, the most comprehensive sanctions regime in U.N. history. On the other hand, I shared membership in the same Order with religious who were suffering at the hands of my own government, to say nothing of the larger Iraqi populace who, of course, I also view as my sisters and brothers.

I was haunted by a comment made by an Iraqi Dominican sister to Timothy Radcliff during his visitation to that country. "The sanctions make us feel that we have been forgotten even by God," she said. Christmas of 1998 was approaching, and the sister's remark brought home to me the heart of that celebration—*it is in the flesh that we learn who God is.* U.S. Dominicans, it seemed to me, had a special obligation to act. Simply writing to Congress wouldn't do. *With our very flesh* we had to say something.

It was a series of very long morning walks that finally led me to place a phone call to Sparkill Dominican sister and friend Eileen Gannon. Knowing that travel to Iraq by U.S. citizens was an act of civil disobedience, with the possibility of serious consequences, I pulled my car over to the side of the road one afternoon, took out my cell phone and called Eileen. "I want to launch delegations of U.S. Dominicans to Iraq. I can't do it alone. Will you work with me on the project?" Without a moment's hesitation, Eileen replied, "Yes."

The first delegation of "Voices for Veritas" went to Iraq in 1999, with two additional ones to follow. The project grew as many U.S. women in the Dominican Family, joined

Voices for Veritas I (February 1999):
Jane Abell, O.P.; Arlene Flaherty, O.P.;
Marilyn Foster, O.P.; Zaïda Gonzales, O.P.;
Jacqueline Hudson, O.P.; Regina McKillip, O.P.;
Ann Marie Rimmer, O.P.; Agnes Schneider, O.P.;
Anne Sullivan, O.P.
Voices for Veritas II (February 2000):
Maira Berry, O.P.; Margaret Galiardi, O.P.,
Eileen Gannon, O.P.; Nancy Goult, O.P.;
Ursula McGovern, O.P.; Marjorie McGregor, O.P.;
Carmen Mele, O.P.; James Nuttall, O.P.;
Mariana Wood, O.P.
Voices for Veritas III (February 2001):
Nancy Erts, O.P.; Gloria Escalona, O.P.L.;
Eileen Meyers, O.P.; Beth Murphy, O.P.;
Roberta Popara, O.P.; Thoma Swanson, O.P.;
Therese Warden, O.P.; Catherine Waters, O.P.;
Rene Weeks, O.P.; Richard Woods, O.P.

by a few of the friars, generously brought their creativity to bear on ways to relieve the suffering of the people of Iraq. I think of those courageous women, joined by a few men, who traveled to Iraq to testify with their very bodies that God forgets no one.

I think also of all the energy put into creative organizing, especially the efforts put forth by Dominicans Laura Somner Coon, Arlene Flaherty, Jane Abell, Mariana Wood, Mary Ellen O'Grady in the Dominican Leadership Conference office; Philippe LeBlanc, who at the time shared with me the position of Co-Promoter for Justice for North America; and Reg McKillip, Beth Murphy, Robin Richard and others too numerous to name. In addition, the support for this project offered to me by Roseanne McHale, Pascal Moffatt, and Anna May Rochford, my staff in the ministry office, was simply superb.

The Dominican Family, both nationally and internationally, was coalescing in prayer, fasting, and action to relieve the suffering of the Iraqi people. Unbreakable bonds were created among the U.S. Dominican women, the people of Iraq, and the Iraqi sisters. As my term as Promoter came to an end, I stepped back and turned this effort so near and dear to my heart over to my successor, Judith Hilbing, O.P. As I write this in the closing days of 2003, Earth herself—through every bone in my body—mourns what the government of the United Sates of America has done to the land and people of Iraq.

All of this happened in conjunction with the responsibilities of congregational leadership. At times, these weighed heavily upon me, no more so than when my mother took ill and died in November of 1997.

Nevertheless, I did enjoy the job. As a colleague once remarked to me, "It's fun to swim around in a bigger tank for a while." The job was particularly challenging for me because my prior ministerial responsibilities found me working anywhere but at the heart of institutions. It was an adjustment to discern just how to bring my gifts and talents to the center of an institution, even if it was my own. As much as time permitted, I read Eco-feminist theology and works about the "New Cosmology,"—the story of the origin and evolutionary unfolding of the universe and the role of the human in that unfolding—and I walked and walked and walked.

Among a number of very fine contributions to the life of the congregation made by our Leadership Team, I took particular delight in our Team's approval, with the affirmation of our Congregational Assembly, of a Community Supported Agriculture (CSA) project on the motherhouse grounds. Initiated by one of our sisters, Jeanne Clarke, it was and remains a great joy to see this project flourishing. Sophia Garden, as it is called, offers people the opportunity to purchase a "share" in the garden's harvest of organically grown produce.

BEING LED TO THE QUEST

It became increasingly clear to me, as my years in leadership progressed, that all the things I could speak about with no one I was able to take with me, during my long walks, "onto the Earth." Earth was supporting me. I did not yet realize, however, that Earth was also beckoning me.

From the day I had been elected to serve as Director of Ministry, I knew that I would serve only one six-year term. In fact, our Constitutions make this the norm. They do, however, leave open the possibility for serving a second term in another capacity.

As we began to prepare for the election of our next Leadership Team, many of our sisters asked me to make myself available to serve as Prioress. My own ruminations on the matter told me this was not the way to go. The obligations and responsibilities were time-consuming and demanding. The energy output required was always high and, more often than not, stress was the name of the game.

I longed for some unscheduled time for myself to allow for the refreshment of my own creativity and dream life. Even more, I longed for periods of prayer when the demands of the job would not intrude upon me. Nevertheless, the requests to make myself available for leadership kept coming. While I did not want to ignore the requests of my sisters, I was quite unsure that a positive response to the call was the best thing for either me or the congregation.

Throughout my years in Leadership, I was a regular visitor to Crystal Spring, an "Ecological Learning Center" in Plainville, Massachusetts. I made all my retreats there and found Chris Loughlin, O.P., one of the Kentucky Dominicans on staff, to be an insightful listener and splendid companion on the way. Earlier I had shared with Chris my fascination with what is called, "A Vision Quest." I wanted to make one after I completed my term in office and had a chance to rest. Another friend, Passionist Sister Gail Worcelo, had participated in a Vision Quest as she sought to discern the foundation of a new religious community devoted to responding to the suffering of Earth. As I was talking to Chris about whether or not to make myself available for the Prioress position, she said, "Too bad you can't make your Vision Quest now."

That's all I needed to hear! It was December of 1999.

ENCOUNTERING MYSTERY
IN THE WILDERNESS

Through experience, I have learned that there are certain things—usually very significant ones—that both attract and frighten me at the same time. That was my initial reaction to the "Vision Quest."

PART ONE: THE VISION QUEST

A Quest is a ten-day experience. The first three days are spent preparing; the next three and a half days are spent in solitude and fasting; and the last three and a half days are spent processing the experience. I learned from Anne Stine, a well-respected Vision Quest guide and founder of Wilderness Rites, Inc. (who was later to become a deeply valued friend and mentor), that the term comes out of the Native American tradition and that it is a rite engaged in at transitional moments in one's life.

Though it is frequently referred to in the context of the transition from adolescence to adulthood, it has applicability to other key points in one's life journey. I felt I was certainly at such a point. I was fifty-four years old. If I were to be elected Prioress, I would be sixty when I completed the term. There was nothing specific that was calling me in another direction, other than an instinctual sense that this was not the way to go. No doubt I was standing with Robert Frost at that very spot where, "Two roads diverged in a yellow wood." I knew that "way would lead on to way," and that choosing one, "I doubted if I should ever come back."

The decision was highly significant. I wanted to honor the sisters who were calling me forth; I wanted to honor my own instincts; most of all I wanted to make a decision out of my deepest self.

With admittedly meager information about "Questing," I scrambled to find out if any were being offered in the immediate future. Time was of the essence—our process of election called for a decision about whether I would make myself available for election by late January. It was approaching mid-December.

> "I am going to the desert to fast and pray to find out what is required of me at this point in my journey."

Through my contact with Anne I learned that a colleague of hers was sponsoring a Quest from December 29 to January 6,

2001. I made the initial inquiry and learned that there was a spot open but that I would have to act very quickly if I wanted to participate. All the while, to quell a low-grade anxiety, I was thinking, "So what's the big deal, I have made many a ten-day retreat in my life."

I soon learned that the Quest was very different from a traditional ten-day retreat. It all came via e-mail from Dave Talmo, founder and lead guide of Wilderness Reflections. Several things "upped the ante":

(1) The entire experience is held outside in the natural world. I had never lived outside, day and night, for ten consecutive days.

(2) One fasts for three days and three nights. For a variety of reasons I had never "gotten into" fasting—to say nothing of a seventy-two-hour fast.

(3) The experience was to be held in the desert of Death Valley, California. This meant that at a given point in the experience I would have to walk a good distance away from the group and set up camp in the middle of the desert with only a tarp, sleeping bag, water, and journal. I would remain there for three days and three nights.

Instinctual fear in the face of a challenge was something I had grown accustomed to. My feelings on reading that e-mail from Dave were sheer terror. After printing the message, I shut off my computer and went outside. As I walked and walked, I wondered: Can I do this? Should I do this? Why *would* I put myself through such an ordeal? Clearly, this was very different from a "standard retreat."

Gail Worcelo was the only person I knew who had actually "Quested." I called her to chat. It was reassuring to speak with someone who had returned alive! Chris Loughlin, whose off-hand comment prompted me to investigate the possibility of going on an immediate Quest, was a great support to me in dealing with the initial terror. Most significantly, she called my attention to the fact that it was I who responded to her comment. She reinforced this by reminding me, "that is how close to the surface all of this is within you." I made my decision. My attraction to the Vision Quest experience was greater than my fear of it. I was going!

PREPARING THE WAY

A flurry of activity followed. Some of it was in the middle of the night! I was waking up repeatedly. Moving through me in a darkness that was fertile was the realization, "I am going to the desert to fast and pray to find out what is required of me at this point in my journey."

I turned to the Scriptures and repeatedly read through Jesus' experience of prayer and fasting in the wilderness. More powerful than any particular thought about or insight into Jesus' time in the desert was the realization that I was about to actually live through a similar experience.

At this time, synchronistically, I was reading Sallie McFague's newest book, LIFE ABUNDANT: RETHINKING THEOLOGY AND ECONOMY FOR A PLANET IN PERIL. In the preface she notes a plea of St. Augustine's that appears in the early part of his CONFESSIONS:

> *For thy mercies' sake, O Lord my God, tell me what Thou art to me.*[1]

Significantly, I recognized this as more foundational to my upcoming Quest than simply whether I should make myself available for election. It tapped into the Scriptural question, "What are you going out into the desert to see?" The full import of all of this was yet to unfold.

During the day (in addition to work responsibilities), I was occupied with gathering a long list of things required for the experience: warm winter clothing for the evenings and light summer clothing for the days. (We were, I was told, to expect a fifty-degree range of temperature—from thirty degrees at night to eighty degrees during the day.) I needed a sleeping bag, a small backpack, a whistle, a therma-rest mat, a tarp, an emergency blanket, and four gallons of water to drink during the fast. I was to bring a plate and cup, silverware, and a bandanna. An inconsequential note on the information sheet mentioned that I also needed a large backpack, back-packing boots, and the ability to carry a thirty-to-forty pound pack about a mile. I was in reasonably good shape but I had never done anything like that!

So I began wearing a backpack filled with books during my early morning walks to increase my stamina. Imagine the sight of a middle-aged woman, wearing backpacking boots and a large pack, traipsing around the streets of Brooklyn early in the morning. I was lucky I wasn't arrested! I made my plane reservations, and borrowed as much of the required equipment as I could. On the morning of my fifty-fourth birthday, I sent off my check to confirm my spot on the Quest.

The "coincidences" that occurred during this period were striking. As an example, the orientation material stressed the importance of communicating with one's closest friends regarding the Quest experience. Have a party, they suggested! Weeks before, I had invited my friends to celebrate my birthday. Now they came bearing items I would need for the Quest, graciously allowing me to borrow them. I can still remember Val's demonstration of how one handles a full-sized backpack and what to do with the all the strings and clips.

My local community was fantastic, especially when the only tent I could borrow was for five persons and the trial run for putting it up took place in the middle of the living room! (Thanks to Maureen,

Bern, Kathie, and Anne.) Later, on arriving in Death Valley, Annie Bloom, the lead guide, would take one look at my tent and say, "I wouldn't recommend your using that!"

The orientation material also mentioned that it would be particularly helpful to give one's friends the dates of the "solo" part of the experience—the time spent apart in prayer and fasting—and to ask for their prayerful support. I was so terrified at the thought of this solo time that I was *begging* for prayers from anyone I thought would not have me committed for getting myself involved in this scheme in the first place.

OPENING TO AN EARTH-BASED SPIRITUALITY

There was yet another dimension of the preparation, by far the most significant one, for it would open up for me what I have come to call Earth-based spirituality.

The preparatory materials required that all prospective participants ("questers" in the Vision Quest language) engage in a daylong "Medicine Walk." We were instructed to spend this day out-doors, on the land, fasting if possible. It was suggested that we decide where to spend the day ahead of time, preferably at a spot where there would be no people around. We were to make every effort to be outside by sunrise and to remain there until sunset. The material suggested we sit, walk around, explore, go off the beaten-track, but not read. Journaling about our intention for participating in the Quest was encouraged and it was suggested that the land, wind, and water, the birds, trees and flowers might inform our intention for questing.

Deciding on a spot presented some minor challenges since I was living in an urban area. Safety was also a concern of mine. But these were easily surmountable as my early morning forays had resulted in my discovering a number of lovely spots that were not too distant from where I lived. As for safety issues, I decided I would use my common sense and push against the fear.

I was curious as to why this experience was being called a *Medicine* Walk. I learned (in one of a long line of learnings) that in the Native American tradition, "medicine" is anything that improves one's connection to the Great Mystery and all of life. This would include the healing of body, mind and spirit....Native American medicine is an all-encompassing 'way of life,' for it involves walking on the Earth Mother in perfect harmony with the Universe."[2]

I didn't know it at the time but my first Medicine Walk began the process of integrating much of what I had learned from studying the New Cosmology with an experiential intimacy with Earth. (This is an exciting and vivifying process which I hope will continue to unfold.) Through this process, I would learn to befriend my own fears in a different way and a whole new world would open up for me.

I set out for my first Medicine Walk on a cold and snowy December day. I planned to spend the time on the shores of Blue Heron Pond in Staten Island, New York. It was a spot I had visited many times and I felt both safe and secluded, since it is both set back in the woods and surrounded by private homes.

Deep morning silence and a slate-grey sky, heavy with snow, greeted me as I got out of my car and began my trek around the pond. As I walked through the woods and approached a nearby foot bridge, I was lost in the healing silence and quietly falling snow. The pond was partially frozen and the clearing ahead caused me to raise my eyes, or so I thought. Instantly, I realized it was the presence of a Great Blue Heron in flight, in all of her majesty, not more than twenty feet ahead of me, that was summoning my attention. I simply stopped and, to use Brian Swimme's term, "gawked." Gawking, says Swimme, is a distinctively human activity. It occurs

when "an item of consciousness fills a human—no activity is demanded just awareness."[3]

The sight of this majestic being in flight more than filled my awareness; it was an epiphany of blessing and encouragement for my upcoming journey. It was also the beginning of my love affair with this magnificent being.

Journeying onto the land with deep attention in the manner called for by the Medicine Walk was both strange and comforting for me. I had always loved the outdoors but must honestly admit that it was the pressures of leadership that consistently drove me outdoors and helped me to discover that there were companions waiting to befriend me in the natural world. I did not yet recognize that without them, as Thomas Berry says, there is no spiritual life.

Clearly, I was at home with the silence; it was the inclusion of the larger community of life *as* companions and carriers of revelation that felt a bit unfamiliar and even uncomfortable to me. This experience of discomfort actually became painful as I proceeded to identify what are called my "totem animals." Authors Sams and Carson explain,

> As you come into this Earth Walk, there are seven directions surrounding your physical body. These directions are East, South, West, North, Above, Below and Within.... You have a "totem" animal in each of the seven directions to teach you the lessons of these directions.[4]

Totems are symbolic animals to which, in the Native tradition, a person is related. While I enjoyed the medicine card ritual through which I discovered my connection to rabbit, porcupine, hummingbird, deer, weasel, coyote, elk, owl, and the blue heron, I also was in touch with what felt like irritating questions such as, "What *am* I doing? Is this one big gimmick?" And even the way-down-deep "whispered" question: "Is this pagan?"

More than a "head trip," I found these queries created the sensation of a physical tearing in my body. I now recognize these questions as sheer gift—the re-membering of my life's journey was beginning. It was through these questions that I was to touch within myself a deeply buried alienation from the natural world. The full impact of this became clear to me months later as I awakened in my sleeping bag on the ground in California's Inyo Mountains. But that would be August of 2001. It was now December 28, 2000, and I was on my way to Death Valley.

INTO DEATH VALLEY

Equipped with a full-size backpack and duffel bag, I made my way to JFK Airport for my flight to Las Vegas. While wandering around the airport waiting for the plane, I was hit with the realization, "It is your possible election as Prioress of which you must let go." I made a mental note of the flash of insight and completed an easy trip into Las Vegas. Upon arrival I found my way to a local motel and met up with two other questers, Michelle and Karen, a mother-and-daughter team. They had made arrangements for a car rental and we were to drive together early in the morning into Death Valley.

As we approached the area, I sank further and further into the back seat of the car. I was simply awash with wonder. Having been born and raised in the city, I had never seen such an achingly beautiful landscape. I would later write, "Death Valley is beautiful beyond anything I have known. Engulfed in a silence that is profound are acres and acres of desert, canyons, washes, and mountains, all of which the sun colors a thousand different shades throughout every turning of Earth we call day."

Death Valley National Park is located in southwestern California, just three hours from Las Vegas. It has more than 3.3 million acres of spectacular desert scenery, interesting and rare desert wildlife, a complex geology, and undisturbed wilderness. It is one of the hottest places in the world. It takes its name from the 156-mile-long north-south trending trough, Death Valley, that formed between the Amargosa mountain range on the East and the Panamint range on the West. Telescope Peak, the highest peak in the park and in the Panamint Mountains, rises 11,049 feet above sea level and lies only fifteen miles from the lowest point in the United

States—the Badwater Basin salt pan, some 282 feet below sea level.[5]

Arrangements had been made to meet the group at Stovepipe Wells, one of several campgrounds within the boundaries of the park. Karen and Michelle and I arrived on schedule, shortly before 10 a.m., and introduced ourselves to the rest of the group. Annie Bloom was the lead guide and Jen Shurtliff her assistant. The other questers were John and Daniel. John was a young dad; he and his wife had just had their first child. Daniel was a college student in his late twenties.

Before I realized it we were well into the preparatory stages of the quest. It was hot, eighty degrees or so. We were all in shorts, wearing hats and sun screen to protect ourselves from the desert sun beating down on us. We were joined at the hip with our water bottles, as drinking is essential to avoid dehydration.

We sat in a circle most of the day. First came the ice-breaking activities to get to know one another a bit, and then the guides began a series of activities to focus us on our intention for questing. I always have some concern about revealing my choice of lifestyle in this kind of situation, partially because of the impact it has on others and partially because I find it tiring to deal with others' projections about nuns. There was no choice in this situation. I simply could not do the work I had come to do without sharing my membership in a religious congregation. To my delight, in the ten days I was with the group, a comment about it was made only once.

One evening Daniel, without thinking, had brought some food to his sleeping area. In his absence, Coyote had come and raided it. Known as the "Tricksters" in Native American lore, Coyote are not very discriminating. Along with the food, they took his wallet, containing hundreds of dollars, and some other personal belongings. In an effort to help Dan regain his possessions, we spread out over the entire area in search of his things. His wallet was recovered. I was the lucky one, however, to find his underwear. Howls of laughter resonated throughout Stovepipe Wells, as Jen exclaimed, "Oh, sure! The nun finds the man's underwear!"

Although the beauty of the place was unparalleled, I was aware as evening approached of a growing anxiety. I never went camping as a child. In my early days in the congregation, several of my friends and I did some camping up north along the coast, but I had never slept out under the stars. I was out here for the next nine days and nights—dare I say "stuck" out here?—in the middle of the desert! What if this whole thing doesn't work for me?

Earlier that morning, members of the group had commented on how unexpectedly cold it had been the night before. I absolutely detest being cold! Topping it all off, Annie kept pointing to the mountains surrounding the desert floor on which we were to sleep for the next three nights: "There, those mountains way off in the distance, that's where you will go to fast."

> The desert landscape began to work on me.

I must confess to thoughts of hitching back to Las Vegas and getting out on the next plane! I remember thinking to myself that I had done a lot of crazy things but this one seemed to take the cake.

SHOW ME, GOD, WHO YOU ARE TO ME

The desert landscape began to work on me. My first night under the stars brought a very significant dream. Through the exquisite language of symbol and imagery, a dream about the death of a male friend's mother shed light on both the origin of my fears and my ability to transcend them, offering all the assurance I needed to know I was in the right place. It was only for me to enter into the experience. Rising early in the morning, I walked around the campground. As if to confirm my dream, I was gifted with my first sighting of a Raven. Only later, as I apprenticed myself to the natural world, would I learn that "Raven" brings the gift of courage to enter into the "the darkness of the void, which is the home of all that is not yet in form."[6]

As our wonderful and sensitive guide, Annie, led us in one experience after another to sharpen our focus for questing I began to notice that the issue of making myself available for Prioress was shifting, much as the desert sands do with the slightest wind. Somehow I was more focused on my rendering of Augustine's request, "For your mercies sake show me, God, who you are to me and [only secondarily] what you would have me do." This somehow deeply touched in me the more foundational question, "What are you going out into the desert to see?" It was to this question that I felt more drawn.

With Annie's expert guidance we were sent off on yet another Medicine Walk. I learned more of the significance of this practice as she and Jen began to explain the "Medicine Wheel" or, as some call it, "The Earth Wheel." In DANCING WITH THE WHEEL, I read:

> Forms of the Medicine Wheel exist all around the globe from the great stone circles of Europe to the mandalas of India. All of these are reminders of our past when the world was guided by the law of right relationship and humans respected themselves and all their relations—mineral, plant, animal, spirit—on the Earth Mother.[7]

The Medicine Wheel is based on the primordial Earth-Sun relationship where the numinous energy in each of the four directions is discerned. Hence:

> **South**, the place of the noonday sun, is the summer, the place of fullness of growth, the place of the child, the body and play.
>
> **West**, the place of the setting sun, is the place of darkness, of descent into mystery where one goes inside to discover the true self.
>
> **North**, the place of dark and cold, is the place of the ancestors, the place where one is challenged to survive for the benefit of the whole, the place where one learns an intelligence that is based on the flourishing of all beings and future generations.
>
> **East**, the place of the rising sun, is the spark of creation, the birthing place and the place of fulfillment and illumination, the place where the split between the sacred and the profane is healed.[8]

Only in retrospect do I recognize the Medicine Wheel and practices emanating from it, such as "The Prayer of the Four Directions" and "The Medicine Walk," to be foundational in re-building a sense of what it means to be human in the twenty-first century.

Perhaps this point is most clearly made by recounting a conversation I had with a friend. I was explaining my new learnings about the wheel and the four directions and she replied, "Well, that is a very interesting theory. Did the Quest guides make it up themselves?" As I reflected on this conversation, it came home to me that her question signaled the larger societal loss of connection

> *What are you going out into the desert to see?* It was to this question that I felt drawn.

with Earth and its rhythms. Not only do we not see ourselves, as humans, as manifestations of the life *of* the planet, we have forgotten that we depend on the natural world and that everything is based on this dependence. I think this is what Thomas Berry means when he says, "The Earth is primary; the human is derivative."

WALKING THE FOUR DIRECTIONS

These learnings, however, were embryonic as I set out on my second Medicine Walk.

As I walked East, I asked to be shown what was being born in me and how I was to be inspired. I noticed immediately that the actual pathway to the East was strewn with rocks and the walking was anything but easy. It was late afternoon and the sunlight bouncing off the mountains shrouded the road in deep shadows. The way to greater insight is never easy and more often than not, it demands negotiating some tricky pathways with less light than one would desire. Yet the sand dunes and the Amargosa Mountains spoke to me of gentleness and stillness. I sighed deeply. My work with both the congregation and larger Dominican Order had taken me many places. It was time, it now seemed, to sink roots deeply within the Earth.

As I walked toward the South, asking to be shown the fullness of life, the valley itself, surrounded by mountains, took on the appearance of a life-giving womb of enormous proportions. The nourishment it offered was rich and deep beyond measure and very alluring; yet the immensity of it, curiously enough, struck a note of fear within me.

I tried to play with the fear. My memory called me back to theologian Sallie McFague, who also happens to be a hiker. "On the trail, we humans fit into nature, we can feel comfortable in our proper place."[9]

I hardly felt comfortable. I remembered scientist and author Ursula Goodenough's experience. After having learned in a physics class about the immensity of the universe and its chaotic "violent" dynamics while in her twenties, she went on a camping trip. As she says,

I found myself in a sleeping bag looking up into the crisp Colorado night. Before I could look around for Orion and the Big Dipper, I was overwhelmed with terror. The panic became so acute that I had to roll over and bury my face in my pillow.[10]

It was my recollection of Denise Levertov's poem, "The Beginning of Wisdom," that finally brought me back into some kind of equilibrium:

You have brought me so far.
                    O
I know so much. Names, verbs, images. My mind
overflows, a drawer that can't close.
                    O
Unscathed among the tortured. Ignorant parchment
uninscribed, light strokes only, where a scribe
tried out a pen.
                    O
I am so small, a speck of dust
moving across the huge world. The world
a speck of dust in the universe.
                    O
Are you holding
the universe? You hold
onto to my smallness. How do you grasp it,
how does it not
slip away?

O

I know so little.

O

You have brought me so far.[11]

As I encountered the Western landscape, I noticed an extensive area of what appeared to be baked sand or clay. Its hard and brittle appearance seemed to call me into the work of the West: going into the dark to discover what the true self is trying to communicate. I wondered about my fears. True, I had always pushed against them. Yet here they were again, creating a kind of internal brittleness mirrored by the baked sand at my feet.

There was an added dimension to the fear I experienced in the desert, though. It made me angry. How had I, who had spent significant childhood years playing in the natural world, become alienated from it? I wanted to feel at home here and yet, if the truth were told, I didn't. I bent down to take some of the baked sand in my hands and much to my surprise it dissolved upon touch! I resolved on the spot to continue to move forward in opening myself to deeper experience in the natural world. There was an unmediated presence of Mystery being offered to me here that challenged me to embrace my fears much as I bent to take the desert sands into my hands. It appeared to be a critical complement to my intellectual studies of the New Cosmology.

I had been walking for while and was tired as I moved toward the North. Strong in my newly taken resolve, I began to wonder how all of this would fit into the wisdom of the ancestors in my own faith tradition. As I walked, I noticed that there were a variety of "bushes" on

> How had I, who had spent significant childhood years playing in the natural world, become alienated from it?

the desert floor. Some seemed vibrant even though it was winter; others were in a stage of dormancy; while yet others were clearly dead. I began to notice the differences among them. I came upon a patch of dead ones. They grabbed at the leg of my slacks and almost made me stumble. "Noticing" appeared to be the operative word: Take from the tradition that which is alive, but leave that which is dead to its own process of transformation, or else you stumble trying to do something beyond you which rests in the larger powers of the universe.

As I returned to camp I felt a little like a child who had just completed her first reader, for in fact that was what I was learning to do—to read the revelation of the natural world. Something resonated deep within as I began thinking of the Medicine Walk as the origin of *Lectio Divina*.[12]

The quest progressed and before I knew it, the fast had begun; the next morning we were on our way to those mountains to which Annie was continually pointing. As we traveled deeper and deeper into the wilderness (reminded of this fact by small signs marked, WILDERNESS), I was nearly overcome by the healing power of the landscape. The expansiveness, simplicity, and even harshness appeared to be "washing a numbness from my soul"[13] that I didn't even know existed. I was later to write:

> Simple white and green sign
> I have never seen before
> Says:
> Wilderness.
> The mountains say:
> Wilderness
> My heart leaps!

SOLO TIME: Day One

I had earlier selected a lovely spot (called the "Power Place" in Vision Quest language) for what is called "the solo time" part of the Quest. It was about twenty minutes from base camp and surrounded on three sides by mountains. It was both enclosed and open. In some ways it had the looks of Stovepipe Wells but was a smaller version of the womb-like landscape that was initially both alluring and frightening to me.

Mother Nature had lined the footpath to my Power Place with a lovely bush that I learned is called Desert Holly. It has a striking resemblance to Christmas holly, but with smaller berries and lighter green leaves. It was a nice reminder of the Christmas season, which the rest of the world was celebrating while I was traipsing around in the desert!

I reflected on what transpired within me when, the day before, for safety reasons, I had reported back to Annie and Jen the location of my spot. I found myself saying, "I have been waiting all my life to do this." To this day, the only sense I can make of those words is that I had always wanted to make a thirty-day retreat. It symbolized for me a unique and profound encounter with Holy Mystery. For reasons beyond my understanding, it was the Vision Quest to which I was led…and I was not to be disappointed. In fact, for reasons I also cannot understand, I feel that for me the Quest was the encounter I had been waiting for all along.

I marked my Power Place by placing two items on the site. The first is the only thing I have left from the traditional long white Dominican habit—the crucifix I held in my hands as I pronounced my first vows. The second was a pair of prayer beads I purchased on my trip to Iraq. On these beads, the faithful Muslim recites the ninety-nine names of God found in the Koran. Legend has it that there are really a hundred names for God, with the final name known only by the camel—hence the perpetual grin on the camel's face! I set out my sleeping bag at the base of a small hill. I was to be there for the next three days and nights, fasting in solitude.

Annie and Jen had prepared us well for this part of the experience. We had been given all sorts of safety tips and been assigned a "buddy" we would check in with each day through unique arrangements of stones at a predetermined place called the stone pile. This would assure our safety without a face-to-face meeting with another human.We had also been warned to be vigilant for danger signs regarding the fast. Hunger and weakness were to be expected. Repeated vomiting on the other hand was a sign to come in for food. It was instilled in us that fasting is not an endurance test but rather a means to an end. All of this was set against the background of a poem by thirteenth century Sufi mystic, Rumi. Annie, who has a wonderful voice, sang it to wake us the morning we set out for the solo time:

> The breeze at dawn has secrets to tell you.
> DON'T GO BACK TO SLEEP.
> You must ask for what you really want.

DON'T GO BACK TO SLEEP.
People are going back and forth
across the doorsill
where the two worlds touch.
The door is round and open.
DON'T GO BACK TO SLEEP.

Initially, the fast created a clarity of mind and sharpness in me that I had never experienced before. I had made many a retreat but I was here because I wanted Earth to teach me who God was for me and what path I should follow. I wanted to grow in Earth consciousness. That was clearly the reason for the Quest. As for the decision to make myself available for Prioress, it became crystal clear that my life's passion is being Dominican. My love of the congregation and respect for my sisters had confused the question of making myself available for Prioress. I now knew that the only Vision Quest agenda remaining around the question was to mourn the "no"—what it means to close off any possibility in our lives. I ritualized this using the sacred elements of desert sand and wind. I was free now to pursue the real agenda of the Quest.

The first hours of the solo time were easy. I was occupied with such matters as setting up my camp site and sitting in wonder as evidence of the Earth's turning was revealed in the sun's "travel" across the desert sky. The mountains were magnificent.

Everything is asleep in the desert at the end of December, so there was a symphonic performance of surround silence that was stunning and soul stirring to this audience of one. Things really started to happen as evening approached the first night I was by myself in the desert.

As darkness fell so did a sense of apprehension within me. I talked to myself. I knew that lying down on the desert floor in the darkness increased my vulnerability. Yet, I remembered all the people who were praying for me. I thought of my mother's body lying in the Earth. As I asked for protection, I could hear her asking me why I had ever done something as crazy as this! I lit a candle that my friend Maureen had given me and was sinking into the twilight telling myself that everything would be just fine.

Then I heard a sound.

I picked up my flashlight, which was close at hand. There, not ten feet in front of me, was a Kit Fox standing at the end of my tarp, staring in my face! I panicked.

"Oh, my God, go away, go away, go away!" I exclaimed.

It looked at me as if to say, "Who is this strange creature going crazy in front of me?" I was too stunned to move and so was the Fox. This standoff could not have lasted more than a minute or so when finally the Fox blinked and moved. I honestly do not remember what happened next, but it wasn't long before I remembered Annie telling us that such a visitation from the natural world is a great gift.

Well, there was no doubt that I bungled that one! By this time it was dark and I decided that the only sensible thing to do was to get into my sleeping bag, zip it up, and hope that whatever happened next would occur while I was asleep!

SOLO TIME: Day Two

I slept through the night waking with morning's first light. I soon learned that those first hours before the sun "rises" are actually the coldest. I inadvertently had made things a bit harder on myself by selecting a spot surrounded by mountains. This would delay my direct experience of the sun until about 8:45 in the morning.

I quickly established the routine of getting up, seeing to the necessary amenities (such as they were!!), putting on some heavy clothes, and wrapping myself back up in my sleeping bag while I journaled, writing with my gloves on. Later that morning, I explored the area around my camp site.

As I walked, I discovered a rather large creosote bush with an equally large hole at its base. "I bet this is the Fox's hole and *I* am in *its* field," I said to myself. My choice was either to move my spot or share this space with the Fox, if *it* would have *me*. I resolved to stay and be more welcoming should it return the second night.

Return it did. I awakened in the middle of the second night to hear it walking around my tarp. I stayed calm but turned in the sleeping bag to make sure the Fox knew that this "lump" in *its* field was alive. As I lay there waiting to see what would happen, it pressed its snout into the bottom of my sleeping bag, nuzzling my feet. Automatically, I sprang into a sitting position, which, of course, frightened it away.

My first real struggle with hunger came during the night as I completed the second full day of the fast. I dreamt of a steaming plate of my favorite pasta—followed by tray of scrumptious pastries! Yet another dream left me with the question, "Will you follow a direct path or will you meander?"

SOLO TIME: Day Three

I awoke to a weakness I had never experienced, even in illness. I wrote in my journal, "I am very hungry. I feel weak and sick and I am freezing." (Your body temperature drops when fasting.) Annie warned us about this and spoke of this weakness as sheer gift. Lack of physical energy brings a dissipation of resistance on every level. One has no choice but to lean into the weakness and see where it takes you.

The weakness took me to a heightened state of awareness, which manifested itself in different ways. Initially, the mountains that surrounded me began to take on a kind of numinous appearance and, in particular, I felt a unity with the mountain to my East. I wrote in my journal, "It is as if the Eastern mountain has moved into me and we are one." I then recalled that it is only the human with self-reflexive consciousness that is capable of expressing gratitude. Was it grandiosity on my part to express the mountain's gratitude for being? On the other hand, how was I to express the gratitude I felt for sharing, even if fleetingly, in the being of the mountain?

I have heard it said by those who fast for longer periods of time that this practice is as much about the mind as it is about the body. Although I had little experience with fasting, I must have known this instinctively because I kept reminding myself why I was doing this: "For your mercies sake, show me who you are to me."

It seemed that as the weakness increased, so did my feelings of being held by this valley of death, which opened before me secrets of new life. I began to feel like I shared in the camel's secret knowledge of God as, slowly, over the course of the three days, the land offered its response in revelation. *Show me who you are to me…*

I am:
   ~Surround Silence
   ~Terrifying Immensity
   ~Illuminator of the Four Directions
   ~The Sun on Whom You Wait
   ~The Summer in Our Winter
   ~The Life of "Mountain"
   ~Brightest Star of the Desert Night Sky
   ~The One Who Stretches Me Beyond My Fears
   ~The Face of the Rock
   ~Hidden Energy
   ~The One Who Brings Life from a Stone
   ~The One Who Sniffs Out Who We Are
   ~My Dream Teacher
   ~The Changing Colors of the Mountains
   ~The Stark Mountain Peak
   ~The Gently Sloping Hill
   ~Holy Wilderness

It was the third night. The Fox returned, this time simply circling around me as I lay in my sleeping bag.

BACK TO BASE CAMP

On the morning of the fourth day, we were to return to Base Camp by 9 a.m. My physical energy was pretty depleted by this time. I knew the only way I could manage to get my things together and lug them back was to rise early, eat an emergency power bar, and wait for the food to kick in. It was a struggle, particularly to get the backpack on, but I finally managed to do it and get going.

We were warmly welcomed back by Annie and Jen, who skillfully prepared a nutritious yet light meal for four questers who hadn't eaten in seventy-two hours. We broke our fasts together and returned to the original campsite at Stovepipe Wells where the sharing about our time on the land began.

This is a critical piece of the Quest. As each quester shares her or his experience during the solo time, it is

> The gift I was offered by the Kit Fox was an invitation to expand my consciousness to include the rest of the sacred community of life.... It was a call to conversion.

graciously received by the community, and one's experience is "mirrored back," becoming fully confirmed in the self. Annie and Jen handled this part of the experience as expertly as they did all the rest.

When I shared my experience with the Fox, Annie and Jen were wide-eyed. Vision Quest lore holds that any visitation from the natural world is no mere coincidence; rather, the being that appears holds special significance for the quester. For Kit Fox to return each evening of the solo time was truly significant, and Annie and Jen encouraged me to work with its meaning. In an attempt to do so, I wrote:

> Persistent are you little Fox,
> even though my original greeting was less than hospitable,
> three evenings you returned as guest, even nuzzling my feet
> Did you come bearing gifts as guests often do?

It is very clear to me now that the gift I was offered by the Kit Fox was an invitation to expand my consciousness to include the rest of the sacred community of life. "Fox" was reminding me that we only learn to be human by being in relationship to all beings, not simply other human beings. It was a call to conversion.

Early in afternoon of January 6, we said our good-byes and left Death Valley. I knew that I would remove my name from consideration for Prioress. More than that, I did not have a clue.

Nevertheless, I was grinning like the camel!

PART TWO:
GOING DEEPER INTO THE MEANING OF THE QUEST

The experience of the Vision Quest stayed with me in a way that none of my previous retreats did. There was simply loads to "unpack." The end of my term in leadership was approaching. Preparing everything for the transition was a mammoth task that left little time for anything else. Yet I was faced with another significant personal decision.

When I first looked into going on a Vision Quest, it was Anne Stine to whom I was led. We had spoken about my participating in her Apprenticeship Training Program in Eco-psychology, Earth-Healing, and Wilderness Rites of Passage. This was a two-week outdoor program that also included a period of solo time and fasting on the land. Since I had already made a Vision Quest, I questioned whether I should participate in this program. It would occur in August, so the locale was moved to the higher (and cooler) elevations of California's Inyo Mountains, which are northwest of Death Valley.

On the one hand, it seemed too soon for another experience that was so similar. I had my reservations about living outside for *two full weeks*, and this time we would really be out there—at least a forty-five minute truck ride away from *anything*. On the other hand, this program promised to provide an in-depth learning experience. Anne Stine, I would later learn, is a deeply spiritual woman, a pioneer in eco-psychology, and a skilled wilderness guide who has taken hundreds of people out on the land. Much of our time in the mountains would be given over to delving into the meaning behind many of the practices I experienced in Death Valley. It would help me process my Quest and give me time to unwind after six, very demanding, years of ministry. I decided to go.

Dear friend and sister Dominican Patti Bruno graciously opened her apartment in Berkeley to me. It was more than an ideal launching spot for me to connect with the participants in Anne's program, as Patti and I share lots in common. Staying with her immediately before the program (and returning there upon its conclusion) provided prayer, conversation, and good food that was stabilizing and deepening for me (and for her as well, I hope). Her generosity is not to be equaled.

The program turned out to be simply wonderful, and the beginning of unique sharing and friendship between Anne and me. As four car loads of us arrived at Badger Flat in the Inyo mountains, Anne greeted us with, "Welcome home to Earth. You are on the breast of the mother." These words synthesize and summarize everything that was to happen for me in the coming weeks.

There we were: a dozen and a half individual camp sites spread out within the Flat, yet nestled within the larger two million acres of the Inyo

National Forest. The staff had set up a kitchen area. We all brought gallons of water, and necessity would demand periodic trips to town by the staff to procure more. We had our common areas too: a spot designated for gathering in circle, a spot for prayer, a spot for "dining" together. All the comforts of home!

Our daily gatherings began with a morning ritual led either by a staff member or one of the participants. I knew immediately that I did not want to fall into my usual inclination to close my eyes while praying. There in the mountains dubbed "John Muir country," Mother Earth had painted a landscape resplendent in multiple shades of greens, yellows, browns, and reds. Beams of sunlight danced on the ancient rock of the distant Sierra Nevada range. Why would I shut this out? In search of what? This was a place to pray with my eyes wide open. There were other reasons to keep my eyes open—"Rattle Snake" and "Mountain Lion"! Both shared this mountain habitat with us. This was high summer and *everything* was alive. The norm was, "Never put your hands or feet where you eyes have not gone first." Neither made their presence known to us, for which I was very glad.

THE FOUR SHIELDS: AN EARTH-BASED PSYCHOLOGY

Anne began to open up the Medicine Wheel for us in ways that time prohibited during the Vision

Quest. I had the basics down regarding the sense of the four directions. She introduced unfamiliar expressions. Reference was made to East, West, North and South "shields" in the human. I was being exposed for the first time to an Earth-based psychology. Anne explained that the original psychology of the human was based on the premise that we humans *are* nature. I immediately connected this with my struggle to embrace in depth the meaning of the frequently used phrase, "We are Earth conscious, we are Earth reflecting on itself."

Thomas Berry explains this to mean that we humans are

> beings in whom the universe in its evolutionary dimension becomes conscious of itself.... The human person is not a detached observer of this development, but one that is integral to the entire process. Indeed the human may now be defined as the latest expression of the cosmic-Earth process, as that being in whom the cosmic-Earth-human process becomes conscious of itself."[14]

Steven Foster and Meredith Little, founders of the School of Lost Borders, have done the seminal work on the shields in the human in their book, THE FOUR SHIELDS: THE INITIATORY SEASONS OF HUMAN

NATURE.[15] The cycles or seasons of nature are also the cycles and seasons of the human. In nature, spring, the spark of life, is followed by summer's full growth. The dying back we associate with fall is inevitable in any healthy organism; the development of stamina in winter is critical to survival.

> The cycles or seasons of nature are also the cycles and seasons of the human.

This cycle of change, a sign of health in the natural world, is also present in the human. Its absence in either the natural world or the human brings disease. The origin of the rites of passage in the human grew out of the ordeal of coming to grips with the changes in life that are an integral part of this cycle, both internally and externally. Foster and Little say,

> Quite literally we *are* the physical, psychological, mental and spiritual stuff of the seasons. Sometimes we wear the summer face of the child. Sometimes we wear the fall face of the passageway from child to adult. Sometimes we wear the mature winter face of the adult. Sometimes we wear the spring face of regeneration. Usually these faces blend with each other, like summer blends with fall, fall with winter, winter spring, etc.

But no matter how well blended, at any given time one face tends to predominate. That face is the seasonal shield.... If one were looking for mental health, it would involve the ability of individuals to grow into the fullness of each season.[16]

Anne encouraged us to think about the four shields of human nature as a system of immunity; if the shields are all "up and running," *i.e.*, if an individual has access to all four shields within herself, she is healthy.

I struggled with the word "shield." Finally, I arrived at the conclusion that it was simply what I understand to be the "persona," an "announcement" of who a person is.

Every morning, Anne patiently walked us through one of the shields in the human, each based on the primordial Sun-Earth relationship and the subsequent four directions given expression in the Medicine Wheel. She outlined the characteristics of the seasons as lived in each of the four shields of human nature. The afternoons were given over to our engaging in Earth-based practices that would strengthen the particular shield being studied that day.

I soon learned that this system is far more sophisticated than simply identifying the child with the South and summer, the adolescent with West and the fall, the adult with North and the winter, and the enlightened/transformed or regenerated person with East and the spring. Like a wheel turning,

> … summer is the urge of things to be remembered in the fall. But fall's memory must become winter's mind. Winter's mind must give way to the spirit of the spring. The spring must become embodied in the summer. And when the body of summer turns inward to prepare for winter, it falls again into memory. Fall stores away all the memories of the seasons. The memories form complexes within the fall shield. These complexes have a great deal to do with the psychological makeup of human nature.[17]

Earth and its passage through the cycle of the seasons was the *original* paradigm for understanding the human. In the back of my head I once again heard Thomas Berry's words, "The Earth is primary; the human is derivative."

It was fascinating for me to begin to use this lens to understand the peculiarities and even aberrations of human behavior. The theory goes this way: it is possible for a shield to become exaggerated and for an individual to become "stuck." So,

> **If the South is** … the place of summer and play, the place of unrestricted growth, the

place of the body and full instinctual life in the human; **an exaggerated South shield in the human looks like a person who** … suffers addictions of the body, is selfish, and might tend towards ageism.

If the West is … the place of fall, the place of the setting sun, the place of adolescence where one goes inward to do one's work; **an exaggerated West shield in the human looks like a person who** … is unwilling to grow up, is irresponsible, always has a problem, is always a victim and is self-absorbed to the extreme.

If the North is … the place of the winter where Earth goes inward, shuts down and builds reserves for the spring, the place where survival is learned, where in the human one becomes one's own parent, where we willingly control our appetites and instincts in order that others may live; **an exaggerated North shield in the human looks like a person who** … lacks access to the inner life and finds expression in behaviors that are over-controlling, arrogant, rigid, and closed-minded.

If the East is … the place of spring where the hard Earth softens and the spark of new life emerges, where in the human we meet the poet and artist and mystic in ourselves, where our spirituality is grounded, and where we love the body and are in communion with all other life forms; **an exaggerated East shield in the human looks like a person who** … tends toward religious fanaticism and avoids the hard work of the West.[18]

It is also possible to use this system in reflecting on societal ills. Having spent years involved in a multi-systems analysis of war and its causes, I was left speechless hearing war described through this lens as "children in adult drag." Although the expression could be offensive to some, it seemed to capture a truth that many of the other analytical systems missed!

HEALING WAYS OF THE FOUR SHIELDS

Another fascinating aspect of this Earth-based psychology is what is referred to by Foster and Little as "Four Shields therapy." It doesn't take deep psychological disorders for a person to become stuck in a particular shield. The responsibilities of life itself may place demands on us that result in an excessive use of the strengths of a given shield. I experienced this myself.

In August of 2001, when I arrived in the Inyo Mountains to participate in this program, I was tired from six years in leadership and was just beginning to unwind from a job that demanded a strong North shield posture on my behalf. I both wanted and needed to step aside from this and allow myself some space and time. The theory tells us that the way to do this is to move to the opposite shield; so, in my case, it meant moving from the North to the South shield. Of course, the only way to move from winter (North) to summer (South) is through spring (East).[19]

> Earth and its passage through the cycle of the seasons was the *original* paradigm for understanding the human.

Although I was not consciously engaging in this Four Shields therapy, I was aware of my need to let myself relax and even "play" during this Quest experience. Our afternoon experiences provided time for me to do just that. One afternoon we had hours to simply meander in the mountains. On another occasion it was a night walk. Then there was the exploration of flora and fauna I had never see before. I had brought my binoculars and a bird book with me and, much to my delight, the Western mountain birds were showing themselves to me.

One evening I had a dream. In it, a likeness of myself was being sculpted by a male artist. This image and other aspects of the dream communicated a clear message to me. I was to nurture and protect and cherish the "artist" within. From the perspective of the theory, my unconscious was giving me a push Eastward. I responded by becoming extremely careful about doing anything that spoke to me too heavily of the responsible North shield. I vigilantly avoided pushing myself, so much so that I actually ended the solo and fasting time of this experience a day sooner than called for in the schedule.

Two days after this, I had yet another dream. The images spoke of some of the struggle that six years of intensive work close to the heart of any institution brings. It was from this dream that I awoke crying tears of relief as I lay on the ground in my sleeping bag. While the details of the dream were vivid, even more vivid is my memory of the words I found on my lips as I awakened that August morning, "I feel so alienated from Earth. I want this part of my soul back and I will do what is needed (read: "die to whatever I must") in order for that to happen." The experience of being out on the mountain for two weeks just months after my own Vision Quest affected its own therapy for me. I began to move through the death of letting go of much of what was excessively demanding and responsible in the North shield, to nurture the new life that was breaking ground in the East shield.

AWAKENING TO SEVERED CONNECTIONS TO EARTH

In retrospect, I view this as an extremely significant moment. The dream was no doubt what the Jungians call a "big" dream. Sustained reflection on the dream and on two extended periods of living outdoors made me aware of how much of my education, religious formation and socialization as a woman had severed my connectedness with Earth. I began to see my initial dis-ease in the natural world, my awkwardness with Earth-based spiritual practices and my lack of confidence in my ability to take care of myself out of doors, as symptoms of a real amnesia wherein I lost the memory of my origin in the Earth-Mother, as well as my connectedness with "all my relations" in the natural world.

> I need the natural world not simply to breathe and eat and drink...

It was a cold November day months later when all of this took clear form in my consciousness. I was walking in the grey light of late afternoon at the Jamaica Bay Wildlife Sanctuary in New York. A bone-chilling wind was blowing in from the water. No one else was present in the entire park, save a ranger in an office about a mile away. A flock of geese flew overhead. It was so quiet, I could hear the displacement of air affected by

> ...I need the natural world for the life of my soul.

the birds flapping their wings. In a moment of profound awareness I realized, "I need the natural world not simply to breathe and eat and drink; I need the natural world for the life of my soul."

There was no doubt about it. A spring-like spark of new life was effecting a curious re-membering in me. I had an instinctual but very clear sense that I was bringing more of myself to prayer than ever before. At first, I puzzled over this. Finally, I told myself, "Of course this is so; I am, after all, an expression of the multiple life forms of a five-billion-year-old planet, born of the 13.7-billion-year-old universe."

PART THREE: GUIDING OTHER QUESTERS

All of this new life was simply waiting for embodiment in the South of summer when opportunity came knocking. I received an email from Anne Stine, who was inviting me to participate as staff (or "base camp," as it is called) for a Vision Quest to be held in early February of 2002 in Death Valley. I was thrilled to be asked, delighted with the opportunity to learn from such a splendid and spiritual guide, and delirious about returning to Death Valley, the birthplace of so much new life for me.

Initially, it felt odd to be in the role of staff. My own knowledge and instincts about outdoor living were still tender little shoots and here I was assisting others. In spite of this, I felt strong and sure about my insights into the process.

We were a group of sixteen, twelve questers (eight women and four men), two guides, and two base camp assistants. I felt deeply touched as I sat in the circle and listened to the intentions that brought this diverse group of women and men to the desert to fast and pray. Some were praying for life direction; two couples came to celebrate anniversaries; one man was grieving a divorce; one young girl came to mark her passage into full womanhood.

As I looked for ways to be supportive to these splendid human beings, *i.e.*, carrying a pack, lending an ear, assisting with cooking, a woman named Dorcas approached me. We were about to leave to spend the day working on our dreams at the foot of Telescope Peak. I was packing the truck, making sure we had the essentials needed for the day. She seemed somewhat hesitant but clearly wanted to ask me something. So I stopped what I was doing and tried my best to put her at ease.

She said, "Anne told me you are a nun."

"Yes," I replied without hesitation.

"Will you baptize me?"

I was astonished at her request. We talked at length. She had studied the Synoptic Gospels for many years, she told me. Now she wanted to make a public declaration of her love for God. She expressed the deepest desire of her heart—to bring the work and teaching of Jesus, "a vital and living reality," she said, into her life and the world.

Clearly this was not a whimsical request. As our conversation continued, and I listened deeply to her, a single thought kept rising up from the center of my being: "There isn't a reason in the world to withhold baptism from this woman." We were sitting on two big boulders as we talked. I looked around. The snow had begun melting at the top of the mountain, and there, yards from where we sat, a stream was running through the wilderness. After lunch, and some words of invitation from Dorcas to the group, we all gathered at the stream. Dorcas and I stepped into it, and there, in an exquisite and unique stone cathedral, not made by human hands, surrounded by a loving community of questers, Dorcas was baptized.

After completing her fast and solo time, Dorcas would comment on her baptism, "It has changed my whole internal landscape. I always thought I was not good enough for God." Sarah, another one of the questers, said about the baptism, "There was something so very primordial about two women standing together in that stream."

My hands shook once again as I baptized, but this time it was because the water was fr-e-e-e-e-zing! There were also tears again, but these were ones of sheer joy. How could I not remember the last time I had baptized? There, in the wilderness, I whispered a prayer for Bea and Harold and their little baby girl.

On to a New Earth-Based Ministry

Central to understanding the gift of the Vision Quest, is the reality that what is given to the quester is given for the sake of the whole community; the quester, therefore, has a responsibility to manifest it. As Annie said to us as we were preparing to leave Death Valley at the end of my first Quest, "If your vision doesn't grow corn, I don't want to hear about it."

An opportunity to grow corn close to home occurred when Nora Nolty, sister Amityville Dominican and then-Program Director of Siena Spirituality Center, invited me to work with her on re-designing the sabbatical program offered at Siena, an Amityville Dominican-sponsored ministry in Water Mill, Long Island. After extensive conversation we decided to redesign it through the lens of the New Cosmology—the story, as noted earlier, of the origin and ongoing unfolding of the universe, and the role of the human in that unfolding. We adopted a focus sentence against which we would measure every activity of the program.

> Born of our oneness with the universe, the sabbatical will birth transformed images of God, Earth, Self and Others.

In many ways, this sentence grew out of and was a reflection of what I have come to see as the heart of the journey recorded in these pages. To embrace the New Cosmology, both intellectually and experientially, is to open oneself to deeper and more profound religious experience. Everything expands, particularly one's sense of Mystery and the Holy. We realize Earth is "Living" and we learn to read the Earth as revelatory of the Divine. The role of the human is, on the one hand, relativized and, on the other hand, recognized to be more important than ever before.

As with any program, it is from the participants that we gauge its effectiveness. More than twenty women have participated to date and all have been amazed at how life-giving it is to explore the New Cosmology, braided with relaxation, fun, and free time. One woman's comments capture the heart of the experience we intend to offer: "For years I have been looking for a way to go deeper with God and life and I could not find it. This perspective on reality opens up the depth for which I have been searching."

Not long after conducting the first sabbatical program at Siena, I was delighted to take up full-time residence at Siena, as the Center made a commitment "to do" spirituality in the context of the New Cosmology. A special arm of programming reaches out to those with professional expertise in theology and spirituality, seeking ways to re-cast these disciplines in the context of the New Cosmology. The summer of 2003 saw Siena graced by the presence of Canadian eco-feminist theologian Heather Eaton, poet and song-writer Carolyn McDade, and internationally renowned scientist Elisabet Sahtouris. They, together with many fine women and men from all over the country (the majority of whom were Dominicans), probed the insights of the New Cosmology as it seeks to open a pathway into the time when humans and the natural world will live as one mutually enhancing community.

Plans are under way for a spring 2004 program, in which Heather Eaton, Chris Loughlin, O.P., and Cletus Wessels, O.P. will explore the "intersections" among the New Cosmology, religious experience, and the Christian Scriptures. In the summer of 2005, longtime social activist and now "permaculturist"[20] Carol Coston, O.P. and Irish priest and social psychologist Diarmuid O'Murchu will collaborate in bringing their insights to the series.

Other programs, seeking to offer the in-depth religious experience afforded by the New Cosmology to all serious seekers, are becoming more numerous at Siena. Very close to my own heart and, I think a first on Long Island, is Siena's "Wilderness Quest." Designed by me to be a modified version of the Vision Quest, this four-day experience in Long Island's own wilderness is focused on helping people open themselves to the ancient silence, fierce love of Holy Mystery, and sense of awe and gratitude mediated by living on the land. While requiring no previous camping experience, it does include a twenty-four-hour solo experience on the land.

Four women, Carol, Janet, Peggy, and Gail, joined me in pioneering this program during the summer of 2003 on Indian Island in Suffolk County, Long Island. I knew my journey had come full circle

when on the morning of the last day of this experience I heard each of these courageous women speak
in her own way about how a fuller, deeper and richer
sense of herself, Earth, and Holy Mystery was born of
entering the wilderness and living on the land.

A THEOLOGICAL REFLECTION

For me, the experiences I have recounted were extraordinary. I am grateful to my congregation for affording me both the time and the resources necessary to pursue them an in-depth way. Not everyone has this kind of opportunity and some might even ask if it should be offered in light of the many pressing problems at hand in these early years of the twenty-first century.

If you have read the first book in this series, EARTH SPIRITUALITY: IN THE CATHOLIC AND DOMINICAN TRADITIONS, by Springfield Dominican Sharon Zayac, you know that concern for Earth has increasingly found its way into Papal, Episcopal, and Dominican documents of late. Nevertheless, some still relate to the New Cosmology as a "New Age" fad. Is it that? Or is it *the critical reality facing us*? Does focusing on it constitute a desertion, or even a betrayal, of the social justice agenda? Why is it crucial to the study of theology and spirituality in our times? What role does experiential exposure play in all of this?

Perhaps the simplest way to begin reflecting on these questions is by recalling my many visits to the Rose Center for Earth and Space in New York City. If you, too, have had the opportunity to go there, you will recall the brief yet powerful "re-enactment" of the original flaring forth, what scientists call "the big bang." Through the use of modern technology, with its mastery of sound and color, the exhibit opens with a simulation of that moment when time and space began.

After this brief yet powerful experience, you exit onto a ramp leading to a slowly descending spiral walkway that takes you through the ongoing saga of the 13.7-billion-year unfolding of the universe. Every step you take is calibrated, as the entire cosmic story is unfurled.

Your first steps mark the formation of hydrogen and helium. Several more steps place you amidst the formation of the galaxies. As you continue, you note first and second generation stars, with the explosion of one supernova spewing out into the universe all the elements necessary for life. As you keep walking, Earth eventually makes its

> The universe is a text without a context; it is the context of all other texts— and each us was there at the beginning....

appearance. Your final steps mark the evolution of the many life forms of our planet. The extent to which life has developed on Earth, as well as the massive threat that life in its entire splendor now faces is depicted in the Hall of Biodiversity in the adjacent museum of Natural History.

As imaginative and thrilling as this "cosmic walk" experience is, one can easily forget its most basic limitation. Despite the efforts of museum designers to "place us" within what is our *own* story, on some level we may perceive that we have "stepped outside" to observe something *there is no stepping outside of*. In fact, we know that the universe doesn't develop into a pre-existing space. Space and time unfurl *with* the universe, and it is the *whole* that is evolving—not just the creatures and life within the universe.

The universe is a text without a context; it is the context of all other texts—and each us was there at the beginning, in as much as all that we are, in body and spirit, unfolds from that moment of beginning. We are enveloped by this context, we make our way in this context, we ask who we are in this context.[21]

Rather than being some "New Age" fad, the universe and the story of its origin and ongoing unfolding and the role of the human in that unfolding, is *empirically* the basic and ultimate reference point. It is this "given" out of which Earth, the biotic community and the human community, have emerged. A failure to grasp this results in a failure to understand everything. Resistance to probing the implications of the New Cosmology may well represent the single greatest threat to Earth and all of her life forms, including the human. Doing theology or spirituality in a context other than this is strangely akin to choosing to play a grand piano with a single finger.

How Will We Bear It?

In our era where conflict about so many things is the order of the day, Earth and the massive threat to her well being, are a point of convergence for scientist, social analyst, theologian, and poet. Listen to a sample of the thinking:

• Harvard biologist Edward O. Wilson begins his book, THE FUTURE OF LIFE, with the comment,

> The race is now on between the technoscientific forces that are destroying the living environment and those that can be harnessed to save it. We are inside a bottleneck of overpopulation and wasteful consumption....The situation is desperate.[22]

• Canadian theologian Heather Eaton begins her article, "Ecofeminism, Cosmology, and Spiritual Renewal," with the statement:

[The ecological crisis] is understood as the most serious quandary of this, and perhaps of any, human epoch, since a viable future depends upon decisions made by the current generation.[23]

• Poet Wendell Berry writes,

It is the destruction of the world
in our own lives that drives us
half insane, and more than half.
To destroy that which we were given
in trust: how will we bear it?[24]

• The Worldwatch Institute, in their annual STATE OF THE WORLD REPORT, has been documenting for years how the global economy is on a collision course with Earth's ecosystems. The 2003 report states,

The generations who share the planet today are facing a challenge to innovate on a level that may be as profound as the achievement of our distant ancestors.... Depending on the degree of misery and biological impoverishment that we are prepared to accept, we have only one or perhaps two generations in which to reinvent ourselves.[25]

Inherent in these reflections is the understanding that the destruction of the planet means the destruction of the *source* of human life. While this betrays an impoverished anthropocentric view of Earth and her gifts as a collection of objects for human consumption, it nevertheless captures a stark and too-often overlooked truth. Humans, recent arrivals from a geological perspective, are completely dependent on the planet for survival.

If for no other reason than pragmatism, preventing further devastation of the planet is our critical challenge. Since everything and everyone on Earth depends on the planet, Earth's well being demands the highest priority of commitment. Significantly, for people of faith—any faith—the continued destruction of creation by humans, as evidenced by the extinction of species and the pollution of Earth's air and water, is doubly heart-breaking.

MY SOUL LIFE IS DEPENDENT ON EARTH

All that I have recorded in these pages chronicles for me a return to an awareness of my own rootedness in Earth-Mother. Through these experiences, I gradually came to clarity about something that is so basic, it goes unnoticed—at least it did in my own life: *It is the natural world that first awakened my sense of the Holy.* To destroy it is to destroy that which is both incomparable beauty and our life-line to the Divine.

Those daily walks along the water, of which I have no conscious memory, my childhood experiences playing in "the lots" of Queens, of chasing rabbits, catching polliwogs, and wading through patches of reeds, were rites of initiation into wonder and the meaning of the wild. Sitting on the front "stoop" of our family home every evening waiting for the appearance of the first star, and frequent visits with my friends to the ocean as an adolescent were the means by which the natural world awakened in me what I would now call an interior spaciousness, in which I began to be sensitive to intimations of the Divine.

Thomas Berry gives expression to these experiences in the following way:

> Our inner world of genetic coding was shaped by the same forces that created the world about us. Our inner world is integral with this outer world. *Our soul life is developed only in contact with these surrounding experiences. So integral is our inner world with the outer world that if this outer world is damaged, then the inner life of our souls is diminished proportionately.*[26] (Emphasis added)

When my school days approached, I attended St. Margaret's, the Catholic elementary school in our neighborhood. There, like so many children of my era, I began learning the catechism. This added the very necessary "intellectual" component of studying about God, something for which I remain grateful, even to this day. What I now realize, however (*without faulting or blaming anyone*), is that the actual physical development of the neighborhood in which I lived, coupled with my ongoing education in the faith and growth as a young woman, had a profound effect upon my relationship with the natural world. These experiences began to eclipse my sense of intimacy with nature, making it ever more difficult for me, notwithstanding my life-long love of the outdoors, to be sensitive to *the revelation of the divine in the natural world.* I simply stopped looking for it there.

I believe my experience is not unusual. In fact, I view it as one engendered by the culture of the time in which I grew up. Its implications are widespread. It has resulted in both individual and societal behaviors with regard to the natural world that range from a kind of benign

> The Vision Quest shocked me into remembering that I need the natural world to perceive Holy Mystery.

neglect, on the one hand, to the outright rape of Earth-Mother on the other. In retrospect, I can now see that my experience of the Vision Quest and all it encompassed shocked me into remembering that I need the *natural world* to perceive Holy Mystery. Indeed, without it, there is no spiritual life. Destruction of the natural world diminishes the human soul as is evident in the all-too-numerous acts of violence witnessed in the world today.

My Vision Quest experiences effected a kind of "soul retrieval" in me—a real re-membering of the self—that changed everything. The *fact* of my oneness with the universe, known both experientially and intellectually, deepened and altered my perceptions of myself, God, Earth, and others. These changes led me to believe that I needed to pursue a more fundamental justice—a justice that seems to be foundational to every effort to create right relationships.

Earth is a living being and there is a justice that is owed to the planet by virtue of its very being. Earth *is* primary. This is just the way it is. To safeguard the life of the planet as a whole is to safeguard the whole of life. Is it simplistic to believe that if this can be grasped everything will change? I think not. To know Earth as a single living being is to awaken to the realization that we are an *expression* of the life of the planet. This, in turn, awakens the knowing that we are in relationship with *everything* and *everyone* that exists. To know ourselves as beings in relationship with everything and everyone, is to realize that what we humans, unique by virtue of our self-reflexive consciousness, do to Earth and any of its life forms, we do to all life, including ourselves.

This worldview is, most fundamentally, a way of *being* in the single, sacred community of life that has the potential to create personal and societal ways of *doing* that are inherently just. More than urging the performance of specific acts of justice on behalf of humans alone (as good and necessary as this is), it holds the possibility for transforming the sum total of values, beliefs, customs, and ways of behavior toward life in its totality. It is this world-view that seems to me to hold the potential for the radical restructuring of society for which I have been searching.

It strikes me that this is what Jesus was praying for in his utterance, "That they may be one." Rather than a betrayal of social justice, this transformed worldview appears to me to be foundational to the deep conversion necessary so that we "may be one." To build on anything less is to build on sand.

AN ANCIENT PRACTICE FOR THESE NEW TIMES

These foundational understandings would probably never have sunk as deeply into me as they have, if I had simply engaged in an intellectual study of the New Cosmology. Entering into the natural world ("going into the desert to fast and pray") is an ancient spiritual process yet my experience has taught me that it is as important and relevant today as it ever was.

While it was deeply enriching for me to live

> What does seem indispensable to me is that we create spiritual practices that will help us regain a sense of intimacy with the natural world and that will awaken in us its revelation of the Divine.

outdoors for an extended period of time, that kind of intensive exposure to the natural world is neither necessary nor always possible. What does seem indispensable to me, however, is that we create spiritual practices that will help us regain a sense of intimacy with the natural world and that will awaken in us its revelation of the Divine. Some of us may be restricted by circumstances to simply sitting and looking out a window while others may be able to enjoy long walks in the woods. Regardless of the form the practice takes, the essential piece is that it involve communing with the natural world and deeply seeing and experiencing its sacredness.

Philosopher and wilderness guide Jack Turner points out that it is in the natural world that we experience ourselves as an expression of the biological realm.[27] Thomas Berry frames it this way, "There are not two worlds, the world of the human and a world of the other modes of being. There is a single world. We will live or die as this world lives or dies."[28]

Religious experience in these opening years of the twenty-first century simply must be seen as inclusive of the natural world if we are to preserve our Earth-Mother from destruction.[29] Not only do we as individuals need to respond to this challenge, even more critically, so must all institutional religions for the sake of God's beloved and imperiled creation. Along the way, we will find our sense of the Holy immeasurably expanded. At least, this is what happened to me.

AFTERWORD
FROM THE EDITOR

The significance of "encountering mystery in the wilderness" hit home during a week in February 2004, when Margaret Galiardi, O.P. was visiting us at Santuario Sisterfarm. We had spent a good part of the week working on her manuscript, exploring ways to deepen the reader's understanding of her extraordinary experience on the Vision Quest. On the afternoon of her last day with us, Margaret joined Carol Coston, O.P., Ona Lindauer (who, with Monica Gagnon, was one of our first two college interns), and me for a walk by the Guadalupe River, accompanied by our three dogs.

We were less than a mile into the walk when Margaret, who trailed slightly behind with our smallest dog, called out in an urgent hushed voice, "Look behind!"

Not ten feet behind her was a small deer, slightly larger than our sixty-pound dog, who, along with the other two canines, seemed just as stunned at the sight of the so-near deer as we were. As Margaret took a few steps forward, the deer stepped in behind

her. Noticing that Margaret had a camera hanging around her neck, I slowly walked over to retrieve it, and freed her of the leash and dog. While I was engaged in these maneuvers, the deer, incredibly, stayed put; Carol and Ona, meanwhile, took all three dogs and walked ahead, away from us.

The above photo captures what we thought would be the closest encounter between Margaret and the deer. We didn't know, as Margaret put the camera back in its case, that the deer would follow the two of us for the next mile of the walk, coming right up to us at one point, first licking our outstretched hands and then gently raising its front hooves onto each of our shoulders. This is when we confirmed that "she" was a "he." The deer's behavior and touch was so light, however, no hint of aggression or dominance, that I was barely aware of his presence until I felt his soft breath on my ear.

The young deer continued to follow us until we met up with Carol and Ona, who had already turned to begin the walk back home. This time, the dogs did not hesitate to bark and their barking chased the deer over a fence. He continued to follow us until another fence blocked his path; we left him behind, pacing.

A short while later, still retracing our steps back home, we heard the screech of two hawks perched on the highest limbs of the cypresses lining the other side of the river. It was not far from the spot where the deer first began trailing Margaret. One of the hawks took flight. Its red tail caught the waning sunlight as the hawk banked high above. It came to rest on another tree, but not before completing a clean and clear circle around us.

When we got home, we turned to "Deer" in the "Dictionary of Animal Totems" by Ted Andrews. Our eyes widened as we read that deer represent "innocence and *a return to the wilderness*"[30] (emphasis added). Turning to "Hawk," we found these words: "a powerful bird [that] can awaken visionary power and lead you to your life purpose. It is the messenger bird, and wherever it shows up, pay attention."[31]

—Elise D. García, *editor*

NOTES

1 Sallie McFague, LIFE ABUNDANT: RETHINKING THEOLOGY AND ECONOMY FOR A PLANET IN PERIL (Minneapolis: Fortress Press, 2001), p. xiii.

2 Jamie Sams and David Carson, MEDICINE CARDS (New York: St. Martin's Press, 1988), p. 13.

2 Brian Swimme, CANTICLE TO THE COSMOS (The Tides Foundation Video Series, 1990), Videotape 8.

4 Sams and Carson, p. 18.

5 Death Valley National Park (National Park Service) website: www.nps.gov/deva

6 Sams and Carson, p. 101.

7 Sun Bear, Wabun Wind, and Crysalis Mulligan, DANCING WITH THE WHEEL (New York: Simon & Schuster, 1991), p. 2.

8 Anne Stine, unpublished lectures; also for a detailed explanation of the Medicine Wheel, see Steven Foster and Meredith Little, THE FOUR SHIELDS: THE INITIATORY SEASONS OF HUMAN NATURE (California: Lost Borders Press, 1998).

9 McFague, p. 7.

[10] Ursula Goodenough, THE SACRED DEPTHS OF HUMAN NATURE (New York: Oxford Press, 1998), p. 9.

[11] Denise Levertov, SANDS OF THE WELL (New York: New Directions, 1994), p. 109.

[12] *Lectio Divina*, Luke Dysinger, O.S.B. writes, is a "very ancient art, practiced at one time by all Christians ... a slow, contemplative praying of the Scriptures which enables the Bible, the Word of God, to become a means of union with God." [http://www.valyermo.com/ld-art.html] Using *Lectio Divina* in this context, in essence, is to recognize the book of nature as a "sacred text" in its own right.

[13] Carolyn McDade, COME DRINK DEEP

[14] Thomas Berry, "The New Story," TEILHARD FOR THE 21ST CENTURY (New York: Orbis Press, 2003), p. 77.

[15] Steven Foster and Meredith Little, THE FOUR SHIELDS: THE INITIATORY SEASONS OF HUMAN NATURE (California: Lost Borders Press, 1998), pp. 99-100.

[16] *Ibid.*, p. 15 and p. 20.

[17] *Ibid.*, p. 100.

[18] Anne Stine, unpublished lectures.

[19] If this sounds "gimmicky" to you, I can only assure you that as I have worked with it over the succeeding years, it has yet to fail to shed light and meaning on human behavior—my own and others'.

[20] Permaculture is an Earth ethic for sustainable living that Carol Coston, O.P. describes at length in the second book of the "Dominican Women on Earth"

series—PERMACULTURE: FINDING OUR OWN VINES AND FIG TREES (San Antonio: Sor Juana Press, 2003).

21 Brian Swimme, CANTICLE TO THE COSMOS (The Tides Foundation Video Series, 1990), Lecture One.

22 Edward O. Wilson, THE FUTURE OF LIFE (New York: Alfred Knopf, 2002), p. xxiii.

23 Heather Eaton, "Ecofeminism, Cosmology and Spiritual Renewal," EGLISE ET THEOLOGIE, 1998, p. 115.

24 Wendell Berry, A TIMBERED CHOIR (Washington, D.C.: Counterpoint, 1998), p. 98.

25 Chris Bright, "A History of our Future," STATE OF THE WORLD REPORT, 2003, Linda Stark, ed. (New York: W.W. & Norton Company, 2003), p. 5.

26 Thomas Berry, "Christianity's Role in the Earth Project," CHRISTIANITY AND ECOLOGY, Dieter Hessel and Rosemary Radford Ruether, eds. (Massachusetts: Harvard University Press, 2000), p. 128.

27 Jack Turner, "In Wilderness Is the Preservation of the World," MOUNTAIN RECORD: THE ZEN PRACTITIONER'S JOURNAL, Spring 2001, p. 29.

28 Berry, p. 131.

29Thomas Berry speaks about these changes as "the renewal of the Western religious tradition." See Berry, p. 131.

30 Ted Andrews, ANIMAL-SPEAK (St. Paul: Llewellyn Publications, 2000), p. 263.

31 Ibid., p. 153.

RECOMMENDED RESOURCES

These resources and experiences influenced and inspired Margaret Galiardi, O.P.:

Earth, Our Living Planet. Daily encounters through walks, etc., with the possible assistance of guide books to *your local place*.

VIDEOS
    • COSMIC VOYAGE, an IMAX presentation of the Smithsonian Institution's National Air and Space Museum and the Motorola Foundation.

    • SACRED WILDNESS: ZEN TEACHING OF ROCK AND WATER, Dharma Communications, P.O., Box 156 Mount Tremper, NY 12457 (914)688-7993

    • EXPLORING A NEW COSMOLOGY, REFLECTIONS ON THE WRITING OF THOMAS

Berry and Brian Swimme by Miriam
Therese MacGillis, O.P., Foundation for a
Global Community, 222 High Street, Palo
Alto, CA 94301 (800) 707-7932

Music
• Carolyn McDade, c/o Crystal Spring, 76
Everett Skinner Rd., Plainville, MA 02762;
http://www.gis.net/~surtsey/mcdade

• Jan Novotka, 421 17th Ave., Scranton,
PA 18504

Writings of Thomas Berry

Coelho, Mary Conrow. Awakening Universe,
Emerging Personhood: The Power of
Contemplation in an Evolving Universe. Lima,
Ohio: Wyndham Hall Press, 2000.

Poetry of Mary Oliver

Hessel, Dieter T. and Rosemary Radford Ruether,
editors. Christianity and Ecology. Cambridge:
Harvard University Press, 2000.

Annual State of the World Reports. World Watch
Institute. www.worldwatch.org

Beginning in the thirteenth century, a new form of theology emerged in which women, "for the first time in Christianity, took on an important, perhaps even preponderant role," writes Bernard McGinn in the introduction to MEISTER ECKHART AND THE BEGUINE MYSTICS.[1]

"Vernacular" theology differed both in content and audience from the academic concerns of scholastic theology and the biblical commentary of monastic theology. Written not in Latin but in the spoken language of medieval people, vernacular theology "implied a different and wider audience than that addressed by traditional monastic and scholastic theology."[2]

Among those who contributed significantly to the body of vernacular theology were the Beguines, women in Europe who took up a nontraditional form of independent and apostolic religious life beginning in the twelfth century.

Written by nontraditional women in a nontraditional language, the vernacular teachings also came in nontraditional forms.

According to McGinn, "Much of it was expressed in sermonic form, though of many kinds. A wide variety of treatises and 'little books' were employed, as well as hagiography and letters. Poetry was also of significance."[3]

We draw upon this rich thirteenth-century tradition in publishing this series of "little books," written by Dominican women in a vernacular created out of the soil of their experience of living into new ways of being human, at the dawn of the twenty-first century. These new ways of being are impelled by an inchoate awareness of our place in the universe and by the shocking awareness of an imperiled Earth.

The first awareness: In the last quarter of the twentieth century, insights gleaned from new scientific understandings about the nature and origin of our universe have been applied by a host of writers in a variety of fields, including theology, to revisit assumptions derived from a more than 300-year-old understanding of the universe as a static, mechanistic, and hierarchically ordered object. The writings reflect the profound psychic shift we have undergone in seeing, for the first time in human history, our home planet from outer space; in learning about the deep interconnectedness of all life; in reawakening, through scientific inquiry, to the ancient revelation of "Oneness" that all our spiritual traditions teach; and in understanding our place in the universe as a self-aware, conscious species inhabiting a "privileged" planet, where life has emerged through an epic fourteen-billion-year journey that is still unfolding in form and consciousness.

The second: With the public stir created by the publication of Rachel Carson's SILENT SPRING in 1962, as Springfield Dominican Sharon Zayac points out in EARTH SPIRITUALITY: IN THE CATHOLIC AND DOMINICAN TRADITIONS[4], the modern environmental movement began. Since then, innumerable reports, studies, and books have been written, documenting the extraordinary assault on Earth's life systems undertaken by humans during the past 100 years. Life on Earth has not been this threatened since sixty-five million years ago when, as scientists now believe, a six-mile-wide asteroid plunged into the ocean off the Yucatan Peninsula. Dinosaurs were among the many species that went extinct in the ensuing nuclear darkness; it took some ten to fifteen million years for Earth to recover from the disaster.[5]

In response to these signs of the times, many groups and individuals around the globe have begun to act, including women religious. Among congregations of Catholic Sisters, many are approaching their own "motherlands" differently: conserving land, creating wildlife habitat, letting fields lie fallow, converting to organic growing, exploring alternative energy usage. A number of women religious around the world have established ecological centers dedicated to teaching Earth literacy, modeling ways of living lightly on the land, understanding systemic connections of oppression among all forms of domination, exploring Earth spirituality, cultivating diversity, and nurturing sustainable relationships among all creation.

Of the three-dozen or so ecological centers and initiatives that have been created by women religious in the United States, more than one third were founded or co-founded by Dominican sisters (see list on p.104). Best known among these is Genesis Farm, founded in 1980 by Caldwell Dominican Miriam Therese MacGillis, whose inspiring example helped give birth to so many of the other centers.

The authors of this series are Dominican women who, like Miriam and women in other religious communities, are living into and sharing new ways of being human on Earth. Actually, these are ways that indigenous peoples have long known and lived and that all humans are now being called to learn, drawing on their own spiritual traditions, if our species is to survive.

For many Catholics, the unfolding "Universe Story" and "new" Earth spirituality are wonder-filled invitations to go deeper into the mysteries of their faith; to plumb its incarnational and sacramental essence. Teilhard de Chardin grasped the awesomeness of it all when he wrote:

The sacramental Species are formed by the totality of the world, and the duration of the creation is the time needed for its consecration.[6]

Seven hundred years earlier, Beguine mystic Mechtild of Magdeburg (1210-c1280) had intuited this Oneness, writing:

> The day of my spiritual awakening
>   was the day I saw
>   and knew I saw
>   all things in God
>   and God
>   in all things.[7]

More practical than mystical, Sor Juana Inés de la Cruz (1648-1695)—the Mexican nun, scientist, poet, musician, and scholar whose memory is honored by the Sor Juana Press—dedicated herself to "reading" the natural world through observation on the several occasions when she was forbidden to read books. Believing that knowledge of the arts and sciences was the path to knowledge of God, Sor Juana wrote:

> It seem[s] to me debilitating for a Catholic not to know everything in this life of the Divine Mysteries that can be learned through natural means....[8]

It is our hope that these "little books" will stimulate an engaging *conversatio* ("living with a familiarity that includes but is not limited to verbal discussion"[9]) among women religious and others about both the issues each author presents and the spiritual journey she shares. In particular, we hope that each "little book" will stimulate deep *conversatio* around questions of faith, spirituality, and Divine consciousness.

- Editors

[1] MEISTER ECKHART AND THE BEGUINE MYSTICS, ed. by Bernard McGinn (New York: Continuum, 1994), p. 6.
[2] *Ibid.*, p. 8.
[3] *Ibid.*, p. 9.
[4] Sharon Zayac, O.P., EARTH SPIRITUALITY: IN THE CATHOLIC AND DOMINICAN TRADITIONS, "Dominican Women on Earth," ed. by Elise D. García and Carol Coston, O.P. (San Antonio, Texas: Sor Juana Press, 2003), p. 18.
[5] See Tim Flannery, THE ETERNAL FRONTIER: AN ECOLOGICAL HISTORY OF NORTH AMERICA AND ITS PEOPLES (New York: Grove Press, 2001), pp. 9-24.
[6] Pierre Teilhard de Chardin, THE DIVINE MILIEU (New York: Harper & Row, Publishers, 1968), p. 126.
[7] Sue Woodruff, MEDITATIONS WITH MECHTILD OF MAGDEBURG (Santa Fe, New Mexico: Bear & Company, Inc., 1982), p. 42.
[8] Sor Juana Inés de la Cruz, "Response to the Most Illustrious Poetess Sor Filotea de la Cruz," A WOMAN OF GENIUS: THE INTELLECTUAL

AUTOBIOGRAPHY OF SOR JUANA INÉS DE LA CRUZ, trans. by Margaret Sayers Peden (Lime Rock Press, Inc.: Salisbury, Connecticut, 1982), p. 32.

9 See McGuinn, MEISTER ECKHART, p. 8, where he refers to "Meister Eckhart's 'conversation' with the Beguines (understood in the Latin sense of *conversatio*, that is, living with a familiarity that includes but is not limited to verbal discussion)" as providing "a particularly instructive example" of ways in which "medieval mystical texts challenge stereotypes about men and women...."

ECOLOGY/ECOSPIRITUALITY CENTERS
Established by Women Religious in the United States
(Known to the editors as of March 2004)

ALLIUM
LaGrange Park, Illinois
Sisters of St. Joseph of LaGrange

THE BRIDGE BETWEEN
Denmark, Wisconsin
Sinsinawa Dominican Sisters

CEDAR HILL ENRICHMENT CENTER
Gainsville, Georgia
Dominican Sisters of Adrian

CENTER FOR EARTH SPIRITUALITY AND RURAL MINISTRY
Mankato, Minnesota
School Sisters of Notre Dame

CHILDREN'S PEACE GARDEN
Detroit, Michigan
Dominican Sisters of Adrian

CHURCHES' CENTER FOR LAND AND PEOPLE
Sinsinawa, Wisconsin
Sinsinawa Dominican Sisters

CLARE'S WELL
Annandale, Minnesota
Franciscan Sisters of Little Falls

CROWN POINT ECOLOGY CENTER
Bath, Ohio
Sisters of St. Dominic of Akron

CRYSTAL SPRING
Plainville, Massachusetts
Dominicans of St. Catharine, Kentucky

DOMINICAN REFLECTION CENTER
Edmonds, Washington
Dominican Sisters of Adrian

EARTHEART
La Casa de María Retreat Center
Santa Barbara, California
La Casa de María/Immaculate Heart Community
Sisters of St. Joseph, Los Angeles Province
Religious of Sacred Heart of Mary, Western America Province

EARTHLINKS
Denver, Colorado
Loretto Community
Dominican Sisters of Hope

EARTHWORKS
Plymouth, Indiana
Poor Handmaids of Jesus Christ

EVERGREEN
Villa Maria, Pennsylvania
Sisters of Humility of Mary at Villa Maria

FRANCISCAN EARTH LITERACY CENTER
Tiffin, Ohio
Tiffin Franciscans

FRANKLIN FARM
Manchester, New Hampshire
Sisters of Holy Cross

FULL CIRCLE ECOHOUSE OF PRAYER
Port Huron, Michigan
Sisters of Mary Reparatrix

GENESIS FARM
Blairstown, New Jersey
Caldwell Dominican Sisters

GRAILVILLE
Loveland, Ohio
Grailville Community

GREEN MOUNTAIN MONASTERY
North Chittenden, Vermont
Passionist Sisters of the Earth Community

HEARTLAND FARM AND SPIRITUALITY CENTER
Pawnee Rock, Kansas
Great Bend Dominican Sisters

JUBILEE FARM
New Berlin, Illinois
Springfield Dominican Sisters

KNOWLES MERCY SPIRITUALITY CENTER
Waterloo, Nebraska
Sisters of Mercy, Omaha Regional Community

MERCY ECOLOGY INSTITUTE
Madison, Connecticut
Sisters of Mercy

MICHAELA FARM
Oldenburg, Indiana
Sisters of St. Francis of Oldenburg

NAZARETH FARM AND CENTER
FOR ENVIRONMENTAL SPIRITUALITY
Kalamazoo, Michigan
Sisters of St. Joseph of Nazareth

PRAIRIE WOODS FRANCISCAN SPIRITUALITY CENTER
Hiawatha, Iowa
Franciscan Sisters of Perpetual Adoration

PRAYER LODGE
Busby, Montana
Sisters of St. Francis of Oldenburg

RED HILL FARM
Acton, Pennsylvania
Sisters of St. Francis of Philadelphia

SANTUARIO SISTERFARM
Welfare, Texas
Dominican Sisters of Adrian

SHEPHERD'S CORNER
Blacklick, Ohio
Columbus Dominican Sisters

SIENA SPIRITUALITY CENTER
Water Mill, New York
Amityville Dominican Sisters

SISTERS HILL FARM
Bronx, New York
Sisters of Charity of New York

SOPHIA GARDEN AND LEARNING CENTER
Amityville, New York
Amityville Dominican Sisters

SPRINGBANK RETREAT CENTER
Kingstree, South Carolina
Dominican Sisters of Adrian
Sisters of St. Francis of Oldenburg

ST. CATHARINE FARM/DOMINICAN EARTH CENTER
St. Catharine, Kentucky
Dominicans of St. Catharine, Kentucky

WATERSPIRIT
Elberon, New Jersey
Sisters of St. Joseph of Peace

WHITE VIOLET CENTER FOR ECO-JUSTICE
Saint Mary-of-the-Woods, Indiana
Sisters of Providence of Saint Mary-of-the-Woods

THE WOODLANDS
Osseo, Wisconsin
Sisters of St. Francis of Assisi

Note: In addition to establishing ecology and/or ecospirituality centers, women religious in the United States and in a number of countries around the world are engaged in an array of activities aimed at conserving land, promoting sustainable practices, restoring natural habitats, and modeling new ways of living lightly on Earth. Descriptions of a number of these efforts can be found on the website of the National Catholic Rural Life Conference (see www.ncrlc.com) and in the annotated directory of members of Sisters of Earth, a network of women dedicated to healing Earth's community of life, founded in 1994 by a group of concerned women religious (see www.sistersofearth.org). As more centers are identified, we will include them in next publication.

Among the many outstanding examples of ecological efforts underway is the "Ecovillage" project completed in April 2003 by the Sisters, Servants of the Immaculate Heart of Mary (IHMs) of Monroe, Michigan. The IHMs invested $56 million in a massive effort to renovate their 376,000-square-foot motherhouse in an environmentally conscious way, developing, among other things, geothermal wells for heating and cooling and a graywater system for reusing water that will cut consumption by thirty-five percent (see www.ihmsisters.org).

Several communities have established congregation-wide ecology committees, such as the Loretto Community's Earth Network Coordinating Committee, to share information, plan ecology projects, sponsor educational events, and motivate the membership to a deeper ecological sensitivity. Some congregations focus on raising ecological consciousness and practices at their motherhouses. For example, the Earth Stewardship Committee of the Dominican Sisters of Adrian sponsors educational seminars. It also has set up an ecology resource room, coordinated the establishment of a wetlands and a Cosmic Walk on campus grounds, and advocated successfully the switch to chlorine-free postconsumer recycled paper for office supplies.

Others are involved in inter-congregational efforts. In 1998, twelve congregations of women religious, along with other Catholic institutions that own land in the Hudson River bioregion of New York, set up ROAR (Religious Organizations Along the River) to "support one another in using our lands with an attitude of respect for beauty and integrity of Earth" and to "address the interrelated issues of poverty, justice and ecology in this bioregion."